G000272742

How to coach
SQUASH

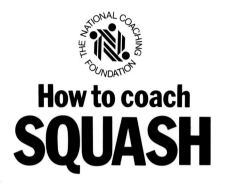

How to coach
SQUASH

Graham Stevenson

WILLOW BOOKS

Willow Books
William Collins Sons & Co Ltd
London • Glasgow • Sydney • Auckland
Toronto • Johannesburg

All rights reserved. No part of this publication may be reproduced
or transmitted in any form or by any means, electronic or mechanical,
including photocopying, recording or any information storage and
retrieval system now known or to be invented without permission in
writing from the publisher.

First published 1990

Copyright © William Collins Sons & Co Ltd 1990

A CIP catalogue record for this book is available from the British Library.

ISBN 0 00 218326 9 (paperback)
ISBN 0 00 218375 7 (hardback)

Commissioning Editor: Michael Doggart
Senior Editor: Lynne Gregory
Designer: Peter Laws
Illustrator: Craig Austin

This book was designed and produced by
Amanuensis Books Ltd
12 Station Road
Didcot
Oxfordshire
OX11 7LL

Printed in China

The pronoun 'he' has been used throughout and should be
interpreted as applying equally to men and women as appropriate.
It is important in sport, as elsewhere, that women and men should
have equal status and opportunities.

CONTENTS

FOREWORD

I first became aware of Graham Stevenson on the squash scene some ten years ago when I presented prizes at a junior event in Brighton. He was the driving-force on that occasion and already wearing a number of his many hats. I was at once impressed with his energy and enthusiasm, attention to detail and obvious skill in communication with both young and old. Not long afterwards he was introduced into the SRA National Junior system and quickly established himself at the core of the élite echelon.

Graham has so many abilities which he can so skilfully transfer to, and instil in, those who work with him. His squash coaching is obviously at the heart of the matter but the success of the National Junior system during this decade is without doubt due in no small degree to his aptitude for organization. That can often be maintained through rigid regard to the rules, but Graham has an engaging sense of humour and an instinctive understanding of when to crack the whip and when to lighten the mood. He is always well-prepared, immaculately groomed and an object lesson in so many ways to keen observers and pupils, both players and coaches.

I would expect this book to be the most thorough presentation, a veritable bible for coaches. The ultimate reference book for those who wish to spread the gospel. And so it is - an immaculate encyclopaedia of excellent advice relating to all aspects of the game. This is not just a guide for potential coaches for it provides so much further room for thought and will provoke constant discussion.

All players too, both at grass-roots and through to the highest professional level, can only benefit from a serious study of this book. There is so much well-illustrated information on practices, preparation (both mental and physical), and such an effective composition of all that is relevant and important, not only to the coaching but also to the playing of the game. Where else can we find such a comprehensive analysis of the primary common faults and the remedies for them?

The younger man of 1980 has learnt his trade well and his work is to be recommended without reservation.

Jonah Barrington

INTRODUCTION

With the boom in the popularity of squash that followed Jonah Barrington's rise to the pinnacle of the game, many books have been written about the sport but they have invariably been player-orientated. To a considerable extent, a player's progress is dependent upon the quality of the coaching advice he is offered, so clearly the coach has an important part to play. It was the realization of this need to raise the general standards of coaching to improve performance in sport that led to the formation of the National Coaching Foundation (NCF). This book, one of the few to be aimed specifically at the coach, is produced in collaboration with the Foundation.

The Collins coaching guides are designed for anyone involved in the introduction of sport to beginners of all ages. In the case of squash, many of the newcomers to the game are youngsters but despite a slight junior bias, the general advice in this book is equally applicable to the coaching of adults. I have written this book with due reference to the various S.R.A. coaches syllabi and to the guidelines so valuably laid out in the NCF Introductory Study Packs - both of which I urge the conscientious coach to consult. My approach has been essentially a practical one, aimed at providing substance and some background theory to the basic framework of the syllabi. Work to expand on these basics has been drawn, very simply, from my experience over the years.

I have long advocated that squash is a game, and games are to be enjoyed, so the philosophy behind this book is very much one of serious effort to do one's best with lots of fun along the way. It is intended to be used as a working manual, so all the main points are summarized at the end of each section or chapter, and the chapter subjects have been chosen to present the information in a logical order.

This book is a compilation of my ideas about the game: some of them original, others borrowed from coaches and players with whom I have been lucky enough to work - but hopefully all will be of value to the ambitious coach who will, no doubt, add many of his own. Although primarily informative, I very much hope that you enjoy reading this guide and that it proves helpful when inspiring your pupils to persevere at improving their squash skill and enjoyment of the game.

Graham

Graham Stevenson

AUTHOR'S ACKNOWLEDGEMENTS

Many people have taught me about the game of squash during my years of playing and coaching, and all have therefore helped to make this book possible. My thanks to them all, with a special note of gratitude to the following:Jane Arkwright, for her assistance with the visual material and patient understanding during the writing phase; Jonah Barrington MBE, for kindly agreeing to write the Forward and for being such an inspiration over the years I have known and worked with him; Malcolm Clarke, who first introduced me to the squash court; John Taylor, for the exchange of ideas during our squad work together; all the staff at the SRA National Junior Squads over the years, especially Steve Draycott, Vivian Grisogono, 'Bomber' Harris, 'Eccentric' Edward Poore,Dr Craig Sharpe and Paul Wright; the squash players of Lancing College, who are often the unwitting 'guinea pigs' for new ideas.

THE AUTHOR

Graham Stevenson is a full-time professional squash coach and and S.R.A. panel tutor. After graduating in Physical Education and Biology from Loughborough in 1974, he taught for two years at Southend School for Boys before moving south to Brighton to take up a management job at Portslade Sports Centre. It was whist at the sports centre that he turned from tennis, his favourite pasttime as junior and student - he played for England U.A.U. - to become increasingly involved in coaching and promoting squash. He was invited to assist with the SRA's National Junior Squad programme from the outset in 1980, and has been very much involved ever since.

From 1981 onwards, he has enjoyed working with pupils of a wide ability range as coach to Lancing College School, so with his responsibilites at county level (looking after the Sussex Under-12's), and as London and Southeast area coach, he is active with all standards of young players. In addition, he has managed England Junior Teams at home and abroad, and indeed has worked with senior and junior players from all over Europe, ranging from complete beginner to national champion. His appointment as an SRA panel tutor, and a recent invitation to sit on the SRA's policy-forming National Coaching Committee means that some of the experience gained in guiding a steady stream of youngsters from novice to National Squad, or even junior international status, is now being channelled into the coaching of coaches.

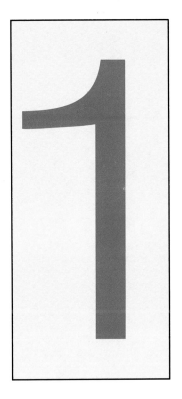

THE ROLE OF THE SQUASH COACH

The Role of the Squash Coach

Perhaps the most obvious question to ask first is 'Why is coaching important?' Surely people will improve just by playing their chosen sport, and by copying its more expert exponents. Why pay to learn? As a professional coach these are questions I constantly ask myself and I highlight them here because the answers appear to me fundamental to the coach's responsibilities.

The desire to improve is general enough to be regarded as human nature. We enjoy success, are frustrated by failure and there are few people who can honestly say they wouldn't prefer to win. Improvement can be made through trial and error, but it takes time. A beginner's instinct is usually to find a short cut to becoming a good player but he invariably finds it difficult to mimic correct technique or to relate to basic tactics. The aim of the coach is easy then: to provide an insight into the essential skills of the game, replacing the player's frustrations of failure with the satisfaction of success.

This is an involved process requiring the harnessing of diverse skills to cope with the diversity of the customer. The fit young man with a burning ambition to get into the top league is an altogether different proposition to the lonely lady who wants to take a course in the hope of making some friends, or the twelve-year-old boy who isn't keen on sports but whose father has high hopes for him.

You'll meet them all and, whatever their natural aptitude or degree of commitment, you will have to cope with them. To do this, consider the coach's Top Ten roles, listed below in a suggested order of importance.

The coach's top ten roles:

1. A Motivator
2. A Squash Expert
3. A Teacher
4. A Communicator
5. An Entertainer
6. An Organizer
7. A Disciplinarian
8. A Trainer
9. An Educator
10. A Role Model

1. A Motivator

Coaching is all about motivating pupils so they want to succeed for the coach's sake as well as their own, and giving them the encouragement to believe that they can do it. If you can develop a pride in practice, your pupils have self-motivation to work even in your absence. Motivation is very much about setting realistic goals and praising good application. Be enthusiastic and your enthusiasm will rub off on your pupils.

2. A Squash Expert

You must be knowledgeable about all aspects of the game but especially the basic technique, tactics and rules. It is essential to be able to demonstrate the basic skills statically, (even if you are not quite so correct under match pressures). Background knowledge of the world's top players and the best local players all helps your credibility and helps generate interest.

3. A Teacher

The ability to introduce and develop new skills is essential. This involves giving a clear, precise description of the skill involved, together with advice on how to master it. In many coaching groups the coach is likely to be coaching not only the pupils to play squash but also showing an assistant how to coach.

4. A Communicator

You must be able to express yourself clearly, introducing enough colour and drama to hold your pupils' attention, and convey your own enthusiasm for the game. Remember, they would probably prefer to be playing a game than listening to you, and your wise words will be falling on deaf ears if you lose their interest.

5. An Entertainer

People learn much better if they are happy, relaxed and enjoying themselves so make your lessons fun. Remove anxiety but keep them on their toes so they are never sure what is going to happen next. If you can act and put on a bit of a show, especially for children, they will enjoy it, remember it and above all, want to come again.

6. An Organizer

You will coach better if you are relaxed and confident. This is easier if you are organized so plan the session, plan the course, set the goals and make the most of every moment. Pupils notice and appreciate a well-organized session.

7. A Disciplinarian

High standards of application and behaviour are essential to success with young pupils both on and off court. Make it just as clear which behaviour you find acceptable as which technique is correct. Do it from the start. Providing you are fair you can still be friendly at the same time. Without order it is impossible to do justice to your squash expertise.

8. A Trainer

Having introduced a new skill it must practised repeatedly until it is 'grooved' and can be relied upon. Very few skills are mastered straight away so the good coach will keep reminding his pupils. Physical training, of the fitness kind, is of secondary importance to beginners, but stretching and movement exercises can usefully be included in their coaching programme (see pages 89-92).

9. An Educator

As a coach you are in a position to influence your pupils' outlook on virtually every matter which arises, and this is particularly so with children. The conscientious coach should realize this because it does carry a certain responsibility.

Take the opportunity to interest the pupils in the National Leagues and news from the various open tournaments. I particularly like to discuss matches in which a player comes back from the brink of defeat or the losing player manages to be gracious in his disappointment. Educate them in competition and teach them how to cope with winning and losing.

10. A Role Model

As the coach you are the centre of attention, so children will tend to follow your example. Your responsibilities therefore include having smart appearance, being punctual, reliable, consistent in your manner (pupils should not suffer just because you are in a bad mood or have a headache), being courteous in your dealings with people around the club and polite to officials when you are playing a match.

However, your responsibilities as a coach do not stop here. If you are aiming for perfection you need to be many other things too:

• An administrator recording attendances, collecting money, organizing leagues and booking courts.

• An analyst identifying the essential skills to be taught. This involves looking at your own game and technique and that of other good players. It's easy to watch two players, but much harder to judge what their real skills are. That takes practice.

• An adviser helping players in the purchase of rackets and other equipment and answering questions like how often a pupil should play and who he should play with. Be ready and make time to help. You will also be asked medical questions and here a coach can quickly get out of his depth. The best advice is always 'If you're worried, see your doctor'.

• An artist who appreciates that playing any game is, to some extent, a means of expression - which is why players end up with infinitely variable styles. However, good technique works so the coaching aesthete may have the edge.

• A diplomat dealing with complaints or sorting out problems. Be nice to get your own way and don't make an enemy of someone, whatever the provocation - you may need his help later.

• A friend. Knowing your pupils helps your coaching considerably, especially when assisting them through the rigours of competitive play.

• A juggler and acrobat. If you don't know what I mean then you haven't had the privilege of trying to keep sixteen under-motivated beginners fully occupied and instructed on four different courts simultaneously. If you can't talk about one thing, think about another, and listen to the next court, whilst looking at your watch and waving to the club proprietor all at the same time, you're a non-starter!

• A physiologist familiar with the physiological changes in the body which are brought about by exercise and training, even if it's just to explain to the player why he is out of breath or tired.

• A politician as, unfortunately, politics and sports are inseparably linked. There will be times when you have to tackle the system or approach the powers-that-be in order to get what you want for your pupils.

• A P.R. man because if you want to be busy or your players want to see their names in the paper, you have got to make it happen yourself.

• A psychologist aware of the traumas attached to winning and losing, coming to terms with a relative lack of ability or coping with an overburdening parental responsibility placed on a child.

• A researcher in touch with progress in all aspects of the game. This may involve going on refresher courses on offer from the Squash Rackets Association (SRA) or the National Coaching Foundation as well as chatting to other coaches and watching the top players in action. Also keep an eye on the equipment shop windows.

• A tour operator as keen players will want to play matches at other clubs, enter tournaments or visit the British Open and you will have to organize it.

• An SRA agent promoting the governing body and making your pupils aware of what it does and offers. Encourage players on your courses to become individual members of the SRA.

• A sociologist maintaining group harmony and understanding the causes of disagreement within your group so you can neutralize the disruptive elements. Be aware if any of your pupils have problems at home - as a coach you might just be the ear which is needed.

Do not be daunted by this formidable array of demands. They are listed simply to help you evaluate your strengths and weaknesses as a coach. Utilize your strengths as much as possible and work on your weaknesses, and remember the aim of coaching which is to help everyone under your guidance to enjoy improving their squash.

THE COACH IN ACTION

The Coach in Action

'On your marks' - Before you start

If you're a professional coach, the reason for coaching is the earning of a living. If you are not, examine your motives. Is it the enjoyment of giving something to the game from which you take personal pleasure? Are you only too happy to help out whilst your son or daughter is involved? Do you like working with children and get genuine satisfaction from seeing them improve? Or is it mainly to feed your own ego, with your pupils simply pawns in your win-for-me approach?

We all have a right as coaches to be delighted when our protégés do well and to feel proud of our contribution to any success they have. Coaches should never, however, lose sight of the fact that they are doing it for the pupil, not for themselves. Coping with success and failure in squash teaches youngsters a good deal about themselves, quite apart from how to hit a squash ball. A good coach sees squash expertise in the context of the pupils' general development and should bear in mind their age and level of ambition. The golden rule is to coach for the pupils' benefit not your own.

Why do people play squash?

One usually assumes that the coaching situation is voluntary and occupied by well-motivated pupils eager to learn. However, that is not always the case and sometimes one's approach has to change slightly to allow for it. Many children, for example, are crazy about sport while others come along because their friend is keen or because their father wants them to play. Clearly some need more motivating than others while some must be treated more gently in order not to put them off.

What do pupils expect of a squash coach?

• Knowledge of the game and experience in playing helps the coach's credibility enormously, though the non-player who

achieves results will nevertheless earn respect and credibility.
• A personality which is friendly, happy, patient, understanding and humorous.
• Authority which is firm but fair.
• An interest in their activities outside of squash and a listening ear when making decisions which affect them as pupils.
• A reaction to performance giving encouragement and genuine praise and, when things go wrong, analysis and instruction on how to correct mistakes. Pupils don't like to be shouted at or ignored.
• Good organization and well-structured sessions. They also appreciate general guidance in the competitive situation.

The important point is that pupils like and respond well to being treated with respect and sensitivity as individuals. You should develop a philosophy of teaching and evolve methods which best suit your talents but have a regard for these feelings.

When should children start playing?

Let children try squash as soon as they show an inclination to, but don't try to coach formally too early. For coaching to be successful they must be old enough to be able to concentrate and understand instructions, otherwise they will be a dangerous and disruptive element in a coaching group. They should also enjoy their efforts at the game. Under-sevens are usually best left to experiment at the game in an informal fashion, but some eight-year-olds can cope very well with a two-hour group coaching session.

There are exceptions, but motor-skill ability is undeniably linked to age. After learning to crawl and then walk, children develop the basic movement skills of running, jumping, throwing, catching and kicking and it is these general skills which are modified into the more specialized sporting skills of a game like squash. The more experience the sooner the skills develop so although the sequence of development remains the same, individuals may consolidate the basic skills at slightly different ages, but usually around six-to-seven-years-of-age. The throwing skill is obviously very important to squash technique as the forehand drive mimics this action quite closely.

Osgood-Schlatter's Disease

Not really a disease, but nevertheless a common ailment in junior squash players, Osgood-Schlatter's disease is characterized by complaints of soreness under the knee-cap, particularly when pushing off a bent leg. It is a problem of the 'growing pain' variety. If it is persistent, and certainly if it is getting worse, it must be rested, sometimes for weeks or even months until the soreness has gone. One of the problems for squash players is that they seldom really straighten their knees, constantly lunging and recovering again, so a good exercise to try to strengthen the knee and hopefully avoid injury is to contract the quadriceps muscle hard whilst sitting with the legs outstretched. Think of pressing the backs of the knees into the floor, and the heels should then lift off the ground - hold for a few seconds and repeat as often as possible.

When to teach the correct technique

As soon as a beginner shows the basic hand/eye coordination to bring the racket into contact regularly with the ball, it is vital to guide him in the correct technique. There will be little consistency in the very early days, but good habits can then be developed from the start and errant technique does not have to be unlearned later

Beware of the 'It will all come good as he gets older/bigger/ stronger' approach; you can guarantee that a youngster will grow, but not that he will become automatically more skilful, and bad habits unfortunately often grow with him.

Guide a pupil towards correct technique from the start.

Caution, children are growing

It is all too easy, particularly when children develop a precocious talent for a sport to view them purely as little adults, oblivious to the fact that mature skills resulting from good coaching may hide a very immature frame which can be damaged by excessive stress. A child's skeleton is relatively soft and cartilagenous. Damage to specific sites on the bone known as growth plates can be serious and long term, so be aware of the dangers of weight training or hard physical work.

Around the age of twelve there is a tendency towards heel pain, up to sixteen knee soreness is often reported and until about twenty back pain can occur (the latter because the spine matures later than the rest of the body).

In mixed groups it is worth noting that girls begin to mature in size before boys and often have a physical advantage around twelve to thirteen years of age. Some pacification of instances of wounded male pride is sometimes necessary as a result.

The adolescent growth spurt leads to what I call the 'Giraffe Syndrome', when problems of poor coordination and loss of speed arise because the limbs increase in length before the corresponding increase in muscular strength. Coping with longer, unfamiliar limbs makes racket skills difficult to master and renders fast turns out of the question so the coach must be patient and encouraging. There is also the accompanying emotional awkwardness which must be recognized and dealt with in a similarly understanding way.

'Get set' - Understanding the Learning Process

Summary
Try to relate the coaching of new skills to the three stages of learning.

If a coach is to teach new skills effectively, it is important that he understands the learning process itself. The learning of a new skill can be broken down into three stages:

1. **The Cognitive Phase** when the pupil tries to understand the basic skills and their relevance to the game situation. A really good introduction, demonstration and explanation of the skill involved is essential at this stage.

2. **The Associative Phase** when the pupil draws upon previous experience in order to attempt a new skill and modify the skills he already possesses. Here the skilful coach offers some insight, hints and tips, for example 'the forehand drive is just like skimming a stone on the water', or relate the new task to a basic skill already learned (see Chapter 3). This phase highlights the value of knowing as much as possible about a pupil's other sporting interests because if you know he plays tennis or badminton, the squash stroke can be explained in terms of modification of these skills.

3. **The Autonomous Phase** when the pupil uses the results of feedback from each attempt to modify and perfect subsequent tries. This will eventually groove the skill until it can be called upon automatically at the appropriate moment in a game. It is during this phase that the coach must show the player exactly what is going wrong, and precisely what must be done to put it right. Video is valuable at this stage. The coach is effectively trying to teach the pupil how to coach himself when he subsequently practices alone. The vital message to get across is quality. Better to do one shot exactly right than ten shots nearly so.

Although it would appear that the three stages are the same for adults and children, adults have more experience to call upon in the second phase and are unlikely to be restricted by any limitations of physical strength (although sometimes lady players are weak in the wrist). I have found, however, that children are less inhibited and are not so embarrassed by failure.

Understanding the beginners' difficulties

How good are you with the racket in the wrong hand? It is all too easy as a coach to take your skills for granted, which can make you unsympathetic to the frustrations that accompany unsuccessful attempts at a skill. By using your wrong hand you will get a very useful insight into the beginner's problems. Give plenty of constructive guidance to help players understand what they are doing wrong and learn from their mistakes. Encourage players who tend to be over-critical of their performance and do not allow them to let one bad shot colour their whole outlook.

The coach should be aware of the disruptive behaviour or apparent loss of interest which may arise from a player finding it hard to accept that he has less ability than someone else. Children below nine years tend not to appreciate the difference between ability and effort, believing that success is dependent purely upon the effort applied. They need encouragement from the coach and must be shown that there is much genuine satisfaction to be gained from improving one's personal performance even if someone else is still that bit better. These players are likely to be the ones who struggle to fit into a coaching group because they are self-centred and need the experience of team work in order to learn to be less selfish. Group coaching can therefore serve these characters, who are usually youngsters, well, quite apart from improving their squash skills.

The good coach will ensure that everyone in his group has some success, even those with the least ability. A boost to the player's confidence works wonders in overcoming one of the greatest enemies of good sporting performance: stress. The more fearful a player is of failure the more likely he is to be tense and do just that. The main counter to this downward spiral is for a coach-generated relaxed atmosphere with lots of sincere encouragement.

It is also important to steer the beginner away from the concepts of winning or losing towards beating his personal record at practice, an achievement of which he can justifiably be proud, irrespective of the performance in relation to others in the group.

A problem which arises with players of any age is negative transfer. There are many benefits in having experience of other sporting activities, but sometimes there is a negative element. The most obvious example is the tennis player whose well-developed hand/eye/racket coordination allows him to hit a squash ball accurately from the outset, but who often suffers from a straight-armed technique which is very difficult to correct. He needs to be carefully shown the difference in stroke technique.

Summary

- Experience learning difficulties by practising with your wrong hand.
- Help young players to evaluate their performance.
- Try to develop constructive self-criticism.
- Encourage teamwork/cooperation.
- Try to ensure that everyone has some success.
- Remove stress by removing the fear of failure.
- Encourage personal records in skills practices.
- Look out for negative as well as positive transfer.
- Ask lots of questions.

Note: A last word on learning/teaching principles

Because the emphasis in beginner squash is on the physical skills of actually hitting the ball, there is a tendency for thinking to stop and 'brain-death' to ensure! The vital stimulus to thought is, I am convinced, to ask lots of questions; having explained a skill fully, make sure your pupils repeat the coaching points by a process of question and answer. The perfect antedote to the junior (or, indeed an adult) who is 'miles away' is to fire a question at him, with perhaps a few press-ups to do if he can't answer it, and twice as many if he doesn't even know what the question is. Providing it is all good-humoured, it always seems to be very well received (children love to see someone 'put on the spot') as well as productive.

'Go' - The Lesson

The coach is now suitably fortified with background knowledge and is ready to meet his pupils on court. Let us first consider the essential elements of any lesson or session and then go on to examine the value of various aids to coaching.

The essential elements are:

1. Warm-up
2. Assessment
3. Introduction
4. Demonstration
5. Explanation
6. Activity
7. Summary
8. Warm-down.

Warm-up

The warm-up is very important but tends to be the most neglected part of the lesson even by experienced players. There are four main values:

1. Prevention of injury. Injury is less likely to happen if the muscles and joints are warm before they have to work or take a load.

2. Preparation of the body for action with the muscles and joints at working temperature and the pulse-rate raised for optimum performance.

3. Increase of mobility/flexibility. In combination with, ideally, a daily stretching regime, it will increases the player's mobility and flexibility enabling him to reach further for the ball and recover better to make the next shot

4. An informal, fun warm-up breaks the ice with new pupils and gives the coach a chance to get to know them.

The warm-up consists of:

1. Joint mobilisation - fairly rapid movements of the limbs and trunk, within the normal range of movement. These include:

• Aerobic/disco type movements to music
• Variations of jogging on the spot with added arm movements
• Skipping
• Court circles including jogging (forwards and backwards), skipping without a rope, sideways strides, touching the floor and jumping to touch the wall. Rowing and swimming on dry land also work well.

The I D E A S model
This stands for:
• Introduction
• Demonstration
• Explanation
• Activity

• A game of follow the leader
• A game of 'float ghost' (stroke-making without the ball).
2. Stretching exercises to stretch the essential muscles, the quadriceps, hamstrings, hip adductors, calf and achilles, buttocks and trunk. A range of flexibility exercises is described and illustrated in Chapter 5 on pages 89-92. All muscle/joint stretches must be done slowly and should be held for a count of ten.
3. Pulse-warming exercises which should be vigorous but for a short period only. Ideas include:
• A one-minute skip
• Thirty squat thrusts
• Twenty court-widths touching the 'nick' each side
• A relay race involving short bursts of skipping with selected circuit exercises (like press-ups or squat thrusts).

Assessment

To get a feel for the level of a group of players, the first time you see them, set them working on a basic skill such as 'chipping' the ball against the wall (see Chapter 4). This will identify any coordination problems, and any left handers who will obviously require reversed instructions. Once you get to know your pupils, it is not generally necessary for you to keep assessing them.

Introduction

This should explain the subject of the lesson to the pupils so they see it in the context of the game and the lessons that may have gone before, or are to come.

Demonstration

Show the pupils the complete stroke and then break it down into three phases: the starting position, point of impact and the follow-through. Play the stroke very slowly and repeat the whole stroke two or three times at the end. Position pupils so they are safe and have the best or closest view possible.

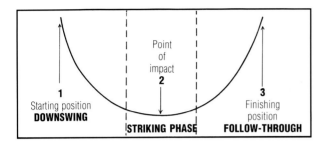

Explanation

Give beginners the main teaching points matching action to words, but don't confuse the issue with unnecessary detail. Include any hints and tips which you know from experience helps pupils to get it right. Also, if possible, describe what the stroke actually feels like: for example which foot carries the body's weight. Encourage the pupils to ask questions.

Activity

Let the pupils have a go as soon as possible, so begin with solo practice, move on to cooperative, and finally competitive pairs work. Make them keep their scores wherever possible, and remember to ask how many they got. Stress the need for quality. It is vital that the coach sees all the players, making quick corrections where necessary and offering lots of encouragement. Get the group together to identify common problems.

While all this is going on the coach might take one court at a time for some feeding and coaching of that group. I always like the final routine or game to involve only two players per court as this is realistic, but take care to keep the rest of a group fully occupied keeping the score or recording errors. A competitive finale combining races with racket skills, provides a good climax to the session.

Summary

Re-emphasize the main points of the lesson and what to practise. I find the ideal time is when the group is occupied with warm-down stretches. If the pupils are really keen to improve, I urge them to make a written note of the advice they receive.

Warm-down

The reverse of a warm-up which consists of gentle jogging or skipping followed by stretching of the main muscles to avoid stiffness developing.

Aids to Successful Coaching

Targets and records

Whenever possible during practice, give the players targets to aim for. Mark a physical target - an area on court marked with insulation tape and encourage players to aim for a numerical target (a personal best for each practice) to beat, which should help concentration.

Physical aids

Sometimes when words and guidance alone have proved inadequate, I have resorted to physical means to achieve correct technique. A floppy wrist can be remedied by binding a crêpe bandage around it. Swinging a skipping rope out to the side to demonstrate circular or centrifugal force has also helped an understanding of the backhand volley sequence.

Video

Video playback/analysis can be enormously valuable with beginners who can see what it is they are doing wrong. There are a few words of video advice, however:
• Spend only a short time with each player: two minutes is plenty
• Allow longer to playback than to record as you will want to repeat parts and play slow motion
• Brief players beforehand about the points of technique to look for, otherwise - particularly if it is a novelty seeing themselves on the screen - they will watch but learn nothing
• Try to arrange the session so that players watch only the relevant parts of the video playback in small groups, otherwise they will quickly get restless

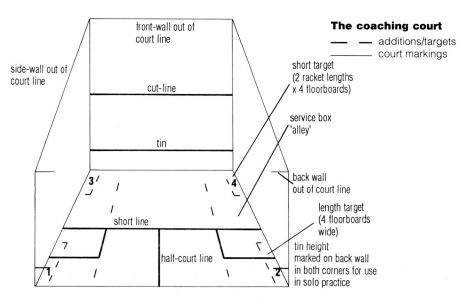

The coaching court

— — additions/targets
——— court markings

front-wall out of court line

side-wall out of court line

cut-line

tin

short target
(2 racket lengths
x 4 floorboards)

service box
'alley'

short line

half-court line

back wall
out of court line

length target
(4 floorboards
wide)

tin height
marked on back wall
in both corners for use
in solo practice

• If there is someone suitable, appoint him your technical operator to leave you free to coach.

Ball machine

Although expensive and occasionally temperamental, the ball machine when properly set up is the perfect feeder of the ball. It is valuable for beginners because a constantly accurate feed allows them to consider one variable at a time during repetition of the same shot. It also helps to 'groove' a technique in a player. Here are some points to consider when using one:
• Point out the dangers. Instruct players never to look into the barrel, never open up the machine unsupervised and never aim it at anyone
• Work players in pairs so one can practise and the other collect the balls
• Introduce movement if appropriate to progress by slowing down the firing action so that the player can return to the 'T' or even ghost another shot between feeds.

• Set up contests between the players and the machine, adjusting the machine to serve.

• Introduce competition by getting each player to count the number of shots per target in a given time or number of goes.

After the Lesson

The fact that a session does not end with the last warm-down stretch can be inconvenient, but the dispensing of progress reports and advice is another important part of the coach's job. Here are some perennial topics of conversation:

Equipment: Players inevitably turn to the coach for advice on rackets, grips, footwear etc. I usually advise them to decide how much to spend and then shop around, looking at and trying all the items in that price range, and choosing what feels right to the player for he must feel happy with it. Note:

• Footwear should have plenty of cushioning in the heel and should not have a pronounced tab at the back. (This so-called achilles protection can in fact press on the tendon and cause soreness.)

• Junior rackets should be used if the junior cannot cope with a full-sized one at the outset. If he can use a full-size racket to chip the ball against the wall with the wrist cocked/racket-head held up, then he should purchase a full-size racket.

Injury and illness: Commonsense should prevail here and, if you have any doubt about the seriousness of an injury, always advise the pupil to get an expert opinion.

• Never let a player exert himself if he has a raised temperature or resting pulse.

• With apparently minor strains, let pain be a guide as to whether a player should continue playing or stop. Avoid pain-killing sprays.

• Use an ice-pack to treat muscle and joint strains and stretch it afterwards.

Parents of young players: Make yourself available to parents and give them reports, discuss how their child is fitting into the group and whether he listens and tries hard. Sometimes it is necessary to spell out to misguided parents who think they have a champion in the making that they have not. More enlightened parents will ask how they can help their offspring on court and you could find yourself with a new assistant for the junior sessions.

THE SKILLS OF THE GAME

The Skills of the Game

The strokes are considered in the order I would tackle their teaching on the court. Emphasis is on the straight shots, as they are fundamental to the game, but the ones which beginners are most reluctant to play because they are more difficult. The section on basic racket control reflects my belief that there is only one fundamental racket skill which, when mastered, facilitates the playing of any shot!

Note: All illustrations and descriptions are for right-handed players; left-handers should simply reverse the instructions from right to left.

The Grip

Unlike tennis or badminton, one grip suffices for all shots in squash, which is just as well since the speed of the game doesn't leave much time to alter it. There is no real advantage in departing from the orthodox or shake-hands grip which is illustrated. The correct grip is fundamental to good technique and racket control, so if a pupil has got into the habit of holding the racket incorrectly, he must be persuaded to persevere and try to change it. Sometimes pupils treat this change to the correct grip as if they are betraying an old friend; tell them it takes time and suggest, if they are already playing league games, they play with the 'old faithful' grip but practise with the correct grip, until such time as they realize the advantage, and actually want to change.

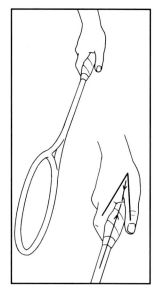

The front of the 'V' between first finger and thumb should be in line with the top left-hand edge of the shaft/grip.

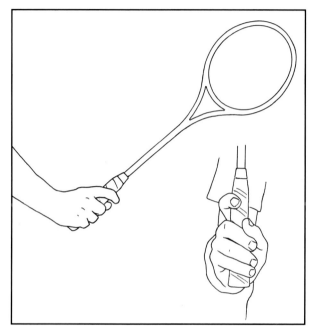

The grip
The index finger 'cocks' the wrist and keeps the racket-head up. The fingers are spread so the thumb is beside the second finger.

Coaching points

1. With the 'wrong' hand hold the racket by the throat and keep the racket-head in the vertical plane Grasp the handle with the correct hand as if shaking hands with it.

2. Spread the fingers with the thumb overlapping the second finger, and the index finger hooked under the grip in order to lift the racket-head when the wrist is cocked.

3. Look down at the grip. The point of the 'V' between the first finger and the thumb should be in line with the top left-hand edge of the shaft/grip so that the forehand racket-face is naturally slightly open.

Controlling the racket
between first finger and
thumb only.

Demonstration

Stand the player or group against the forehand wall and face the wall to demonstrate, holding the racket correctly. Explain with a few shots how the first finger and thumb can steer the racket hitting the ball gently without using the other three fingers.

Show too that the racket-face can be 'opened' on the backhand side, without changing the grip, simply with a slight movement of the wrist.

Fault diagnosis

By far the most common fault with the grip is the tendency to have the grip too far clockwise, with the thumb on the top of the grip. It appears to be a natural position for anyone who has not been shown the correct grip. It leads to a flappy wrist and closed racket-face when stretching to the forehand, and a racket-face which is too open on the backhand.

Hints and tips

• If anyone persistently struggles with the correct grip, try marking their hand and the grip with a pen line so that all they have to do is to check that the two lines correspond (see illustration on page 28).
• With the correct grip, ask pupils to move the racket-head around trying to identify where they can feel the pressure. Pressure should be felt along the index finger and the thumb.
• Tell the players that there is no need to hold the racket too tightly: this can be checked by looking for whiteness on the knuckles. Best results are achieved with a relaxed hand.
• After showing the players the right grip, check and constantly remind them to keep it as the hand will slip back to what feels familiar.
Note: Don't worry if a small/weak pupil wants to hold the racket higher up the grip for better control, although he will, of course, lose power.

Practices

All the solo practices for basic racket control (see Chapter 4), with the emphasis on accuracy rather than power, are suitable for practising the correct grip. (One of the problems in persuading a player to correct the grip is that he can often hit the ball much harder with the 'wrong' grip, at least in the early stages.)

Basic Racket Control

The fundamental factor in racket control which, when mastered, allows the execution of any shot is the use of a cocked but firm wrist to keep the racket head up. If a player can control his wrist, he can control the racket head and thus the ball. This skill, when matched with some tactical ability, can be used to manoeuvre his opponent around the court by hitting the ball away from him.

Many players try from the outset to hit the ball as hard as possible, and even when they begin to drive well, they have little idea what the racket-head is doing. As a result, teaching them the finer points of the game - such as lobs and drops - which require good racket-head awareness, is very tricky. Put the emphasis on accuracy rather than power in solo practices.

Demonstration

Demonstrate at the front of the court, first with pupils against the side wall, and then with them directly behind the line of the racket.

Practice

Instruct the players to stand a distance of about one metre away from the wall and hit the ball slowly against it - this is called 'chipping'. In this way they are practising the vital part of every stroke: the point of impact, as well as strengthening the wrist.

Coaching points

• Check the grip (this is the perfect way to practise using a corrected grip because there is no need to hit hard, or win a rally).
• Keep the wrist cocked using the index finger so the racket-head is up throughout and remains higher than the wrist. When the ball is really low, the knuckles should be the first thing to touch the floor.
• Bend the knees to really get down for the low ones.
• Lead with the left foot on the forehand and the right foot on the backhand. Note that the shoulders are parallel to the side wall.
• Keep the right shoulder as a fixed point and try to take the racket-head back with the racket-face open.
• Lock the wrist, keep the shoulders still, and swing the racket slowly through the ball, taking care to keep the racket-face open.

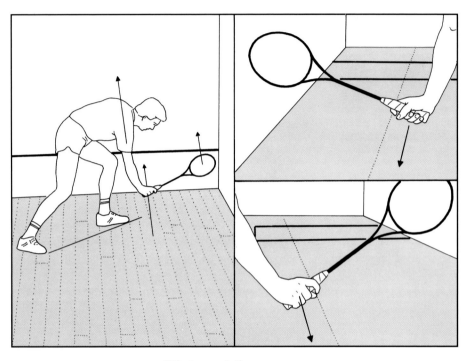

'Chipping' practice
The feet are angled about 45° to the direction of the shot with the hand and racket moving straight through the shot, parallel to the shoulders, with the wrist cocked and the racket-head up.
Top right: With forehand 'chipping' the fingernails are in line with the floor-boards.
Above right: With backhand 'chipping' the knuckles are in line with the floor-boards.

Hints and tips
• Beginners often find it difficult to relate to the racket-head because it is relatively remote. Their hand is much nearer, so get them to think of the fingernails of the racket hand on the forehand going straight through the ball and the knuckles going through on the backhand.
• Encourage them to use the floorboard lines as rails and imagine the fingernails/knuckles running along them when making a stroke
Note: It takes a little while, but once pupils understand the idea, all racket work can be explained in terms of this well-controlled middle phase of the stroke.

Fault diagnosis

Pupil's problem	Likely cause	Coach's advice
Poor control; ball going everywhere	• Wrist flapping	• Cock wrist and lock it as if in plaster
Wrist hurts	• Holding racket too tightly	• Relax grip until whites of knuckles go
Back hurts	• Stooping from waist	• Bend knees to get down
Not enough time between shots	• Racket travelling too fast and swing too long	• Aim higher and stroke really slowly
Ball going into tin	• Racket-face 'closed'	• Turn hand slightly clockwise to open racket face
Ball going into side-wall	• Racket-head dropping and turning	• Cock and lock wrist
Ball going cross-court	• Shoulders too open to front-wall	• Turn more and get leading foot across

SEE PRACTICES FOR BASIC RACKET CONTROL ON PAGE 74

Drives

The straight drive to length is the most fundamental in the game. The idea is to hit it tight - that is, as close to the side-wall as possible - and to good length, so that the ball dies on the second bounce close to the back-wall.

Forehand drive
Coaching points
1. Try to begin from a ready position on the 'T' with the racket-head up.
2. Keeping elbow and wrist still, lift the arm/racket back to the starting position. The elbow should be bent and at least at shoulder height, with the wrist cocked and the racket-head above the pupil's head. The chest will be facing the back of the side-wall and the weight will be on the right leg.
3. Step forwards and across equally on to the left foot. Keeping

The ready position on the 'T'
The racket-head is up, knees slightly bent and the head turned to watch the ball.

Forehand drive

The racket is held up high in the starting position (1). In the down-swing (2) the elbow relaxes and bends and the left foot takes a step forwards and across to the impact point (3). The follow-through (4) should follow the line of the ball and not go across the line.

the elbow bent, throw the racket-head down and out to the side with a relaxed arm, to hit the ball level with the left knee, which should be bent. The shot should be played at a comfortable distance to the side, and with the racket-face slightly open.

4. Keeping the racket-head up (just as in chipping practice), snap the wrist through, but make the racket follow the ball to finish high, with the racket-head pointing upwards not across and the elbow relaxed again. Remember, the follow-through must be safe as well as efficient.

5. Return to the ready position.

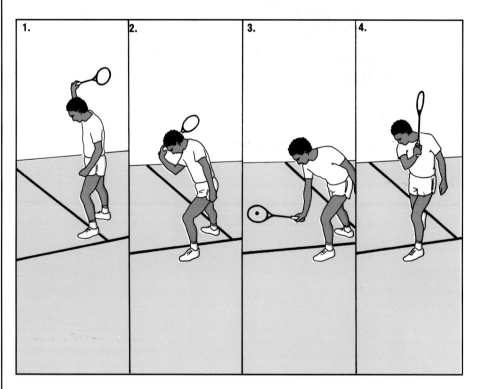

Backhand drive

The backhand drive is the mirror image of the forehand with certain important variations:

Coaching points

1. From the ready position turn the shoulders further than in the forehand drive and step more across than forwards with the right foot.
2. At the same time, lift the racket back high, keeping the elbow tucked in under the hand as the ball is watched over the right shoulder.
3. Aim to hit the ball out to the side and in front of the right foot, with the racket-face slightly opened by pulling the knuckles up towards the forearm.

Drives - hints and tips

• Most problems come from excessive shoulder movement, so tell pupils to keep the shoulders still as they hit the ball and leave the arm to do the work.
• Get the pupils to throw the ball against the wall to practise the correct action. Point out the similarity of the action to skimming stones on water, out to the side and low, not over the top. Follow this up by asking them to throw the racket-head without the ball and finally hand feed the ball for them to actually hit.
• Emphasize tucking the elbow in on the backhand, as this eliminates the problems which arise if it is allowed to drift outwards with the racket-head tipped back over the left shoulder.
• Use the fact that the forehand and backhand are mirror images by getting the pupils to practise them alternately (without the ball), starting one where the other stroke finished. There is no need to move the feet, so the emphasis should be on developing a smooth, relaxed swing/throwing action.
• Stress fingernails (forehand) and knuckles (backhand) through the ball, to ensure a straight follow-through.
• Get the pupils to freeze the follow-through to check the finishing position of the racket.

Demonstrations

• Let pupils watch from the side and from behind.
• Always explain the importance of the follow-through in terms of safety. I stand a volunteer on the 'T' and pretend to play a drive close to him to show that the high follow through is safe, even at close quarters.

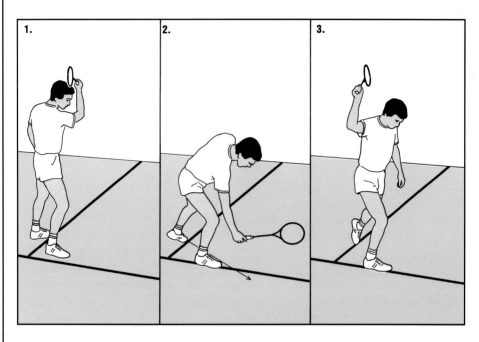

Backhand drive

From the starting position (1) in which the elbow is up high and under the hand, the right foot moves more across than forwards with the racket-face slightly open to the point of impact (2). The follow-through (3) should be high and safe with the shoulders remaining parallel with the side-wall.

Right: At the point of impact the knuckles slightly pull up towards the fore-arm to open the racket-face.

Fault diagnosis

Ball going cross-court	• Hitting too far in front too early • Shoulders swinging	• Remind of correct point of impact • Keep shoulders still by thinking of fingernails/knuckles through
Ball going into side-wall	• Hitting too far back too late • Racket-head being left behind	• Begin earlier to hit ball at correct point • Keep wrist cocked
Missing ball completely	• Poor coordination and timing • Not watching the ball	• Back to racket-control practice • Look for the spot on the ball
Ball going too short/low on F/H	• Closed racket-face • Aiming too low • Finishing too soon	• Check grip • Aim above cut-line • Follow-through high
Over-hitting	• Trying to hit too hard	• Remind of good length; accuracy before power • Aim lower/stroke slower
Stroke looks awkward and player is off-balance	• Swinging in wrong plane • Feet wrong • Arm too straight • Head going down • Too close to the ball	• Start high; finish high • Step forwards and across • Relax elbow • Keep head up and watch ball throughout • Keep 'too far'away
Wild follow-through	• Trying to hit too hard • Too much shoulder swing • Arm staying straight	• Again accuracy first • Try to keep shoulders parallel to side-wall • Relax elbow, to finish forehand where you would start backhand and vice-versa
Ball going too high on B/H with too much slice	• Racket-face open	• Check grip

SEE PRACTICES FOR DRIVES ON PAGE 74-75

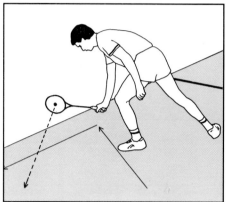

Forehand cross-court drive

Top left: The ball is taken out in front of the left foot in order to hit cross court. (Compare with the impact point for the straight drive, also shown.)

Top right: Looking along the line of the drive, it can be seen how the good width cross-court goes wide of the opponent's racket, and then passes behind him.

Cross-court Drives

The cross-court drive can be used to hit into the opening made when an opponent has been manoeuvred out of position, or to change the direction of attack and make him turn.

Note: I would consider the cross-court only when definite progress has been made on the straight shot because there is a natural inclination to swipe the ball cross-court, and this needs to be countered in the early stages.

Coaching points

The technique is as for the straight shot except:

• The ball should be hit slightly further forwards of the front foot
• The aim should be for the width as well as length, the good width shot striking the side-wall around the back of the service box, so as to be out of reach of the player on the 'T'.

However, if the opponent is caught out of position (i.e. not on the 'T'), it is better to hit the ball direct to the back corner, so it doesn't come off the side-wall towards the approaching player.

Hints and tips

Encourage players to see the side-wall at the back of the service box as a definite target, to avoid the cross-court being aimless.

SEE PRACTICES FOR CROSS-COURT DRIVES ON PAGE 74-75

Volleys

The volley to length is a vital shot for any ambitious player because it puts pressure on an opponent depriving him of time, and forcing him deep into the back corners of the court. It also enables the volleyer to maintain the 'T' position whilst saving him a good deal of running. Most importantly, the volley is the basic means of returning the service. The aim is the same as for the drives: to hit good, tight length.

Forehand volley

Coaching points

1. From the same 'ready position' as for the drives, take the racket back, with the racket-head leading, to the starting position, keeping the wrist and elbow still. Note that the racket-head is tipped back between the vertical and the horizontal plane.

2. Try to step forwards and across on to the left foot (as for the drives) so the body is well balanced and stable for the stroke.

3. Keeping the shoulders still as far as possible, let the elbow lead, to stroke out to the side and strike the ball level with the left foot/shoulder with the racket-head up and the racket-face slightly open.

4. Try to keep the stroke simple with a more punchy shorter swing than for the drives. It is like a chopping action, but directed out to the side, rather than up and down.

Backhand volley

Coaching points

As for the drives, the backhand volley is a mirror image of the forehand except that you:

1. Turn the shoulders further so that the ball is sighted over the right shoulder as it approaches.

2. Aim to strike the ball just in front of the right foot.

3. Keep the head up, especially in the follow-through.

Volleys - hints and tips

• Beginners tend to make the stroke too elaborate, with too many moving parts to the body, so they often run out of time in the preparation and lack control. The answer would seem to be to

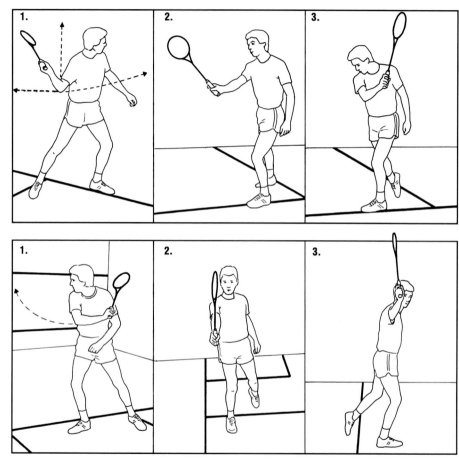

Forehand volley (top)
In the starting position (1), the racket-head is tipped back between the vertical and horizontal plane. The ball is hit (2) level with the left foot with the racket-head up. The wrist is cocked /racket-head up in the follow-through (3).

Backhand volley (above)
In the starting position (1), the racket-head is tipped back and the ball is watched over the right shoulder. The ball is hit (2) just in front of the right foot, with the racket and arm in line. In the follow-through the shoulders stay parallel to the side-wall (3), and the head is up.

punch or chop from the shoulder, keeping everything else still.

• Prevent the volley from being a modified drive, by emphasizing the tipping back of the racket-head, so the stroke is more in the horizontal plane, played out to the side.

• Turn the shoulders in the preparation, not the follow-through. (If the shoulders are not turned enough to begin with, by the time the stroke is started, they will have rotated beyond the parallel to the side-wall, and the shot is unlikely to be hit tight.)

• On the backhand, emphasize the shoulders/elbow/racket-head sequence if the stroke lacks fluency.

• Pupils must be guided towards the habit of volleying.

Demonstrations
Let pupils watch from the side and from behind.

Fault diagnosis

Pupil's problem	Likely cause	Ask the pupil to
Ball going cross-court	• Hitting ball too early/far in front • Over rotation of shoulders	• Wait until ball is in position • Keep shoulders still as ball is hit
Poor control with ball not straight	• Wrist flapping/ ball breaking at impact	• Cock/lock wrist throughout and concentrate on fingernails/ knuckles through ball
Ball hitting side-wall first	• Ball being struck too late/far back, probably because of over-elaborate stroke • On backhand, wrist is bending/ breaking at start of stroke	• Prepare earlier and try to keep stroke short/simple • Cock/lock wrist
Ball landing short of length	• Aiming too low • Racket-face closed	• Aim just above the cut-line • Check grip and remind to tip racket-head
Ball overhit-coming off back-wall	• Too big a swing and too fast	• Shorten swing and think accuracy before power
Dangerous follow-through	• Allowing shoulders to rotate and/or arm straight	• Keep shoulders still, and finish high (hold follow-through to check)

SEE PRACTICES FOR VOLLEYS ON PAGE 76-77

Cross-court Volleys

The cross-court volley is a useful variation which turns an opponent, and can be a winner if hit into the opening created by a straight shot. As for the cross-court drive, I would always work at the straight shot first.

Coaching points

This is as for the straight volley, except:
1. The ball should be hit a little further in front/earlier and aimed for the back of the service box i.e. for width.
2. It can be floated high (racket-head up through the ball), or hit hard and low for the 'nick'(racket-head down through the ball).

SEE PRACTICES FOR CROSS-COURT VOLLEYS ON PAGE 76

Service

The service is the only shot which can be played totally without interference from an opponent, and presents a valuable opportunity to gain an advantage from the start of the rally. It is a good idea to use some variations of service, but first it is essential to perfect a basic serve which is dependable and consistent to present the opponent with a difficult volley, or force him to boast if he lets it bounce.

Coaching points

1. Get well balanced with one foot clearly in the service box and the feet, hips and shoulders carefully lined up in the direction the ball is to travel as illustrated.
2. Look to check opponent's position.
3. Take the racket-head back to the starting position just like that for the volley, but a little lower, at about waist height on the forehand side and a little above on the backhand. Make sure that the racket-head is tipped back so that the racket-face is open.
4. Then, keeping the body still and the wrist firm, stroke slowly up through the ball, remembering to push the fingernails (and therefore the racket-head) through in the desired direction,

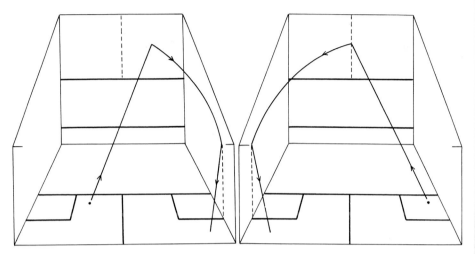

finishing with the racket-head high. Aim about half-way across and about two-thirds of the way up the front wall from the right side (two-thirds across from the left), so the ball hits the opposite side-wall high up just behind the service box. (See above).

5. Keep watching the ball and move to the 'T' with the racket-head up.

Hints and tips

• The correct starting position with the racket back before the ball is thrown, and with racket-head tipped back to open the racket-face in order to impart some cut/backspin, makes all the difference to the shot.

• Pupils must be made to think where the ball is to go, and to aim carefully and place it in the right position on the front-wall. There is a great tendency to just put the ball into play.

• From the left side, it is easier to serve out of the court because of the narrower angle, so encourage pupils to aim for a flatter trajectory by throwing - and therefore, striking - the ball a little higher from the floor, at about shoulder height.

Direction of aim for basic 'height/width' service
Left side: Aim the ball about three-quarters across and two-thirds up the front-wall.
Right side: Aim the ball about half-way across and two-thirds up the front-wall.

Service
Top: Starting position on left and right sides. On both sides the racket-head is tipped back (as for the volley length) and the feet/shoulders are lined up in approximately the direction of the aim.

Above: The service follow-through on the right-hand side. The racket-head (fingernails) follows the desired line of the ball.

Variations of serve
• **Backhand serve from the right side**
The angles/ targets are as for the normal serve from the left side. The advantage is a finer angle with the side wall, making the return more tricky, and the fact that the server is considerably closer to the 'T' (especially useful if an opponent is returning the serve well down the straight wall).
• **Hard, low serve** aimed at the 'nick' and hit hard, rather like a cross-court.
• **Hard-hit serve down the middle**, forces the opponent to turn away from the front wall, and often results in errors or a loose return.

Demonstrations
Let pupils watch from the side, just in front of the service box, and also from behind, where they can look directly along the line of the ball/racket.

Variations of serve
Bottom left: To achieve a flatter, safer trajectory in the left-side serve, throw the ball up a little higher and strike it further from the floor.
Bottom right: The backhand serve from the right side gives a finer angle on the side-wall and leaves the server closer to the 'T'.

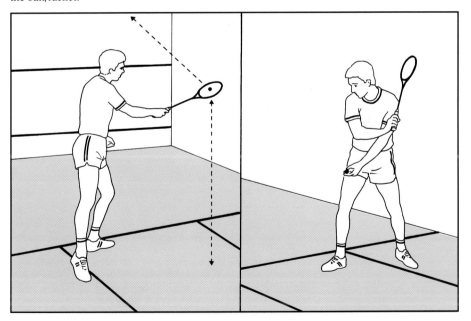

Fault diagnosis

Pupil's problems	Likely cause	Coach's advice
Pupil misses the ball completely (this is surprisingly common)	• Poor hand/eye coordination	• More basic skill work, then practise throwing ball and hitting on to wall from close up
Serve is too low	• Closed racket-face • Poking at ball	• Check grip and starting position • Concentrate on good follow-through
Poor 'width' from right side	• Stance too much towards side-wall • Striking ball too far back	• Line up feet/shoulders in direction of serve • Throw ball further towards front wall
Inconsistent speed and direction of serve	• Not steadying • Wrist flapping • Shoulders swinging	• Check starting position • Keep wrist cocked/firm • Just move arm
Hitting out of court from left	• Hitting too hard so ball is not falling • Wrong angle	• Slower stroke, and use some 'cut' • Check target point on front-wall

SEE PRACTICES FOR SERVICE ON PAGE 77-78

Return of Service

The basic return which a player ought to be able to execute off any serve is the straight-length one, to take the opponent into the back corner furthest away from his service position. If the serve is short or overhit, the receiver can drive the return, but off a good serve, he must volley in order to take away the server's initiative.

Coaching points

1. Stand just behind the service box with feet on the extension of the service-box line, facing towards the side-wall with the racket back at least part of the way. A short pupil may have to stand slightly further back, whilst a tall player or a strong volleyer (which leaves out most beginners) may be confident enough to

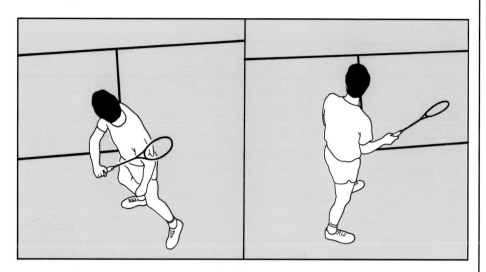

stand nearer to the corner of the service box.

Note: I find that it helps beginners to stand waiting in the position in which they were to hit the ball, so as to keep movement to an absolute minimum.

2. Look for the volley, if possible before the ball hits the side-wall; if not, after it has come clear of the side-wall.

3. Keep the shoulders still and the wrist cocked. Stroke up through the ball to finish high, just as for the ordinary-length volley.

Hints and tips

Keep reminding pupils to volley. Most poor returns are made because the volley is snatched through panic, or failure to realize that the ball will be slowed by hitting the side-wall. Overcome the panic and improve the timing by telling a player to wait until he sees the ball clear of the side-wall before beginning the stroke, and remind him that accuracy should come before power.

Variations

Variations of return occur only too readily with beginners because they are, for the most part, easier, so I concentrate purely on the straight return with beginners.

Preparing for the service return

For both the forehand and backhand the feet are positioned on an extension of the service-box line and the racket-head is back in readiness.

Demonstrations

• A position directly behind the server presents the best safe on-court view of the coach's return.

• On a glass-back court, the view from off-court, behind the receiver (or up on the balcony of a conventional court), gives pupils a chance to look right along the line of the racket/shot.

Fault diagnosis

Pupil's problems	Likely cause	Coach's advice
Keeps leaving ball to bounce	•Frightened of missing ball on volley	•Play a conditioned game where point is lost for not volleying
Tries to volley, but keeps missing	•Playing panicky stroke too early/before ball is there	•Wait, really watch ball and just think of making contact to begin with
Ball goes cross-court	•Hitting it too early and/or the shoulders are swinging	•Again, wait for ball and keep facing side-wall throughout stroke

SEE PRACTICES FOR RETURN OF SERVICE ON PAGE 77-78

Boast

The boast, where the ball reaches the front-wall via the nearest side-wall, may be used defensively to get the ball out of the back corners when it is not possible to hit directly to the front-wall, or as an attacking shot played with the opponent behind the striker. The technique is essentially the same for both. The defensive boast should be used only when it is unavoidable, since it can often present a winning situation for the opponent, or to move an awkward/slow player to the front of the court.

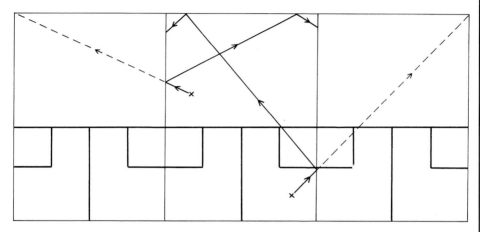

Above: In order to get the correct angle for the boast, aim for the far front corner of the next court. I call this using 'X-ray vision'.

Right: Footwork for the boast. The ideal position for the feet in the forehand (1) and the backhand boast (2), is with the feet lined up in the direction of the shot. When the player is stretched and the ball is behind him, the right foot leads in both the forehand (3) and the backhand (4), and the racket-head is taken back as the player moves.

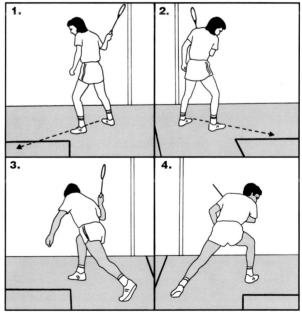

Coaching points

1.The stroke is very similar to that for the drives, but it is necessary to turn the shoulders further, so that they are in line with the direction of the aim.

2. The perfect boast hits the nick and rolls along the floor making it impossible to retrieve. But it is better to make the ball bounce before the opposite side-wall (a two-wall boast), than to overhit it so that the ball comes off the far side-wall into the middle of the court, giving an opponent an easy shot (the three-wall boast).

Note: A three-wall boast hitting low on the far side-wall can be very effective, but because beginners always tend to grossly over-hit, I promote the idea of the two-wall boast which drops into the front-court, right from the outset.

3. The direction of the boast is best determined by aiming to hit through the side-wall, towards the opposite front corner of the next court (see using 'X-ray vision' on previous page).

4. The shoulders should be parallel to the desired direction of the shot as the ball is hit, so players should turn slightly more than this in preparation.

5. Keep away from the side-wall so there is room to swing the racket, and bend the knees if the ball is low, to get under it.

6. If possible, the feet should be positioned as for the drives, but moved a quarter turn towards the back wall. Very often, however, the ball is behind the player, in which case he should stretch back to it with the right foot leading on both forehand and backhand sides. This means he can reach further (because the same arm and leg are leading) and on the forehand side he can easily pivot out to the 'T'again after playing the shot, as described in (8) below.

7. Strike the ball approximately in line with the leading foot with the racket-face slightly open, and stroke lightly up through the ball at no more than medium pace.

8. Follow through in direction of aim using the momentum of the follow-through to help pivot out to the 'T'. The left foot provides the pivot point, with the right coming round towards the 'T'.

Hints and tips

• Some pupils relate readily to the angles of the boast, others are confused. If a player is disorientated, get him to play the boast from a hand feed on the corner of the service box, so he can aim directly across the diagonal of the box to get the correct angle. Hopefully he will then be able to cope with boasting from other positions.

• Most beginners fall into a blind panic in the back corners, so I find it useful to show them how easily the ball can be boasted out slowly and not really aim just by getting under it and aiming high.

• I counter the tendency to overhit the ball by describing the boast as a drop shot via the side-wall (once the drop has been covered), the similarity being the precision required, and the aim of getting the ball to fade away in the front corner.

• Emphasize the fingernails/knuckles through the ball, to counter the tendency to come round/away from the shot too early.

• Other vital ingredients in the back corners are to cock the wrist so as to get closer to the back-wall, and to wait for the ball to come clear of the back-wall before trying to hit it.

• Finally, encourage the pupils to experiment with the height/ speed/angle variables once they can play a boast in basic terms.

Demonstrations

Behind the back-wall on a glass-back court is best for showing the back-corner boast. Failing that, the view from the balcony is useful. Otherwise let the pupils watch from the side and back.

Fault diagnosis

Pupil's problem	Likely cause	Coach's advice
Ball fails to reach front-wall	•Striking side-wall too far back •Aiming too low on side-wall	•Point out correct angle •Bend to get under ball and lift it out
Ball coming off front-wall towards the 'T'	•Striking side-wall too far forwards	•Point out correct angle
Ball coming off opposite side-wall into middle	•Hit too hard and/or too high	•Stroke slower; aim lower
Forehand boast hits tin	•Closed racket-face	•Check grip

SEE PRACTICES FOR BOAST ON PAGE 78-80

Volley Boast

The volley boast can be used as a very effective attacking shot when an opponent is caught behind the striker, ideally on the same side of the court.

Coaching points

• The angles and position of the shoulders are just the same as for the ordinary boast, although in practice there is often insufficient time to move the feet, so the racket is prepared by turning the shoulders from the waist.

• The stroke should be shorter than for the ordinary volley length, there being no need for height or a lot of pace in the shot, and the wrist must be kept very firm for control.

SEE PRACTICES FOR THE VOLLEY BOAST ON PAGES 79-80

Straightening

If possible, the defensive boast should be avoided, because of the danger of 'setting-up' the opponent at the front of the court. Instead, the ball should be straightened, to bring it back to length in the same corner. Good players boast because they choose to: they are seldom forced into it.

Coaching points

1. Keep away from the side-wall to leave room to swing the racket, but get close to the back-wall (as near as the backswing will allow).

2. Face the back of the side wall and take the racket back early, abbreviating the backswing if necessary, and shortening the grip (moving the hand higher up the grip, in effect making the racket shorter) for shots which are very close to the back-wall.

3. Wait for the ball to come clear of the back-wall and bend the knees to get under it, as it will drop low after hitting the back-wall.

4. Keeping the shoulders still, stroke up through the ball, aiming high on the front-wall to bring the ball back tight to the side-wall and to good length.

Straightening by shortening the grip
Opposite right: Forehand. The knee is bent and the wrist cocked. The fingernails should be pushed away towards the side-wall to keep the racket straight.
Opposite far right: Backhand. The knee is very bent and the hand moved to the top of the grip to 'shorten' the racket.

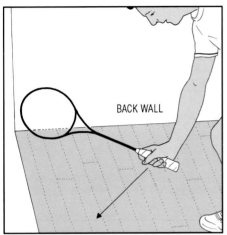

Hints and tips

• Remind pupils that out of the back corner height is their friend.
• On the forehand side the tendency is to bring the racket across the line of the aim, thus dragging the ball away from the side-wall. To counter this, try telling players to push the fingernails away towards the side-wall as they strike the ball and then to follow through.

Demonstrations

From outside a glass-back court, or looking down from the balcony of a conventional court will give the best view.

Fault diagnosis

Pupil's problem	Likely cause	Coach's advice
Ball comes away from side-wall	• Shoulders swinging or wrist flapping	• Keep everything still and push fingernails /knuckles through
Ball hits side-wall first	• Not getting racket behind ball	• Wait longer, untli ball clears back-wall
Shot is hit cross-court when ball comes off back-wall	• Ball is hit too far in front	• Player must move out up the court with the ball, to get alongside it

SEE PRACTICES FOR STRAIGHTENING ON PAGE 79-80

Drops
Below right: In the forehand drop, the feet are lined up in the direction of the shot.
Below left: In the backhand drop, the feet are lined up with the target and the knuckles are pulled up towards the forearm to open the racket-face.

Drops

The drop shot is the perfect complement to the length shot; having forced the opponent deep into the back corners of the court, a weak length or boast can be punished by playing the ball to the front of the court. Even if it is not a winner, it will at least make him run a long way. The straight drop (a forehand hit to the forehand front corner and vice-versa) is safer than the cross-court, because it should finish close to the side-wall, whereas the cross-court which misses the nick often leaves the opponent with an easy winner down the side-wall.

Good players should have a choice between a faster drop played with cut/backspin, or a slower 'pushed' drop, played so the ball fades away in the front corner. The latter is much easier for beginners to tackle, and is, in any case, the better shot when close up to the front-wall. This is because the ball is travelling slowly, and literally dropping on to the front-wall, so it can be aimed higher/safer yet still be very effective (even without deception).

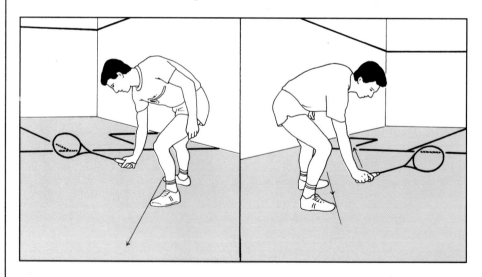

Slow drop
Coaching points
1. Take the racket back early to just above waist height with a short back-swing.
2. Position the body so that the line across the feet/shoulders points towards the direction of the shot.
3. Make sure that the racket-face is open by pulling the knuckles up towards the forearm of the backhand, and by tipping the racket head back slightly on the forehand.
4. Keeping the wrist cocked and still, bend the knees if the ball is low and let the racket swing through slowly, whilst keeping the head and shoulders still.
5. Aim to strike the ball with the racket-face still open, in line with the front foot on the forehand and just in front of the leading foot on the backhand.
6. Stroke right through the ball, with the racket-head continuing to travel in the direction of aim, even after hitting the ball.
7. Aim to hit the front-wall first, so that the ball lands in/near to the side-wall nick. (Providing the shot is hit softly it will still be effective, whether the ball hits low on the side-wall, or lands just short of the side-wall on the floor.).

Drops - the follow-through
In both the forehand (1) and the backhand (2), stroke right through the ball so the racket-head continues in the direction of the aim. The ball hits the front-wall a safe height above the tin and drops into the target area.

Hints and tips
• The key to success is the cocked/locked wrist, so try asking pupils to imagine the wrist is in plaster.
• Again, remind pupils to think of fingernails (forehand) and knuckles (backhand) going through the ball in the direction of aim.
• Emphasize that the swing must be as slow as possible, like an action replay, so the ball actually drops on to the front-wall and stays short, even though it is played with a safe margin for error.
• Emphasize that the follow-through is the insurance against the ball going down - remember 'stroke, don't poke'.

Demonstrations
Hand feed and demonstrate with the player(s) as close as possible to the front corner, and then boast feed/drop with them on the short-line. I also find it useful to show some more drops with them directly behind the racket, in order to look along the line of the stroke.

Fault diagnosis

Pupil's problem	Likely cause	Ask the pupil to
Ball hitting tin	•Racket stopping at the ball •No 'margin for error'	•Push fingernails/knuckles right through •Aim a safe height on front wall
Ball coming back too far off front- wall	•Racket-head moving too fast, and face too flat	•Stroke as slowly as possible with racket-face 'open'(approx. 45°)
Ball good on front wall, but not finishing close to side-wall	•Player not turning/ stepping across enough	•Remember to line-up the feet/shoulders with direction of aim
Ball hitting side-wall first	•Making contact with ball too late/far behind	•Keep wrist cocked/racket in line with arm •Try to hit ball approx. in line with leading foot
Very little consistency	•Too many 'moving' parts complicating the shot	•Cock/lock the wrist and keep shoulders and head still throughout

SEE PRACTICES FOR DROPS ON PAGES 80-84

Long drops

The ability to play the ball in short from relatively deep positions on the court is a valuable one, but it is a shot which requires careful practice if it is not to lead to unforced errors in matchplay.

Coaching points

The stroke for the long drop should be produced in just the same way as the front-court shot, but it requires a slightly higher preparation and follow-through, a wider margin for error and should be played a little faster (so the ball doesn't take so long to reach the front-wall that an opponent has time to get to it). Since the racket should be open as for the ordinary drop, but is travelling faster, more backspin or cut will be produced and this will help to make the ball die.

Hints and tips

Although the shot is played a little faster than one at the front of the court, still stress accuracy before power. To this end encourage pupils to steer the ball short, rather than just to hit it.

SEE PRACTICES FOR LONG DROPS ON PAGE 82-83

Cross court drops

As a variation of the straight shot, to penalize an opponent caught out of position, or if you are confident that it can be a winning shot, drop the ball cross court. It should be noted however that like most cross-court shots, it carries a greater risk if it is not quite accurate enough, since it often leaves the striker out of position.

Coaching points

The technique is just as for the straight drop, except that the ball should be struck further in front/earlier. The follow-through must be towards the far front corner, and the aim is to land the ball in or near the nick or leave it shorter, so that the second bounce is in the nick - either works well.

Hints and tips

Think of hitting across the front wall, rather than down for the nick as this tends to reduce the number of tins.

Note: Deception - To keep things simple, and because a well-executed drop played with the opponent out of position will be a winner, even if he knows where it is going, don't introduce the idea of deception at an early stage. As players become more competent, however, they can practise playing the drop from a gradually higher starting position, so they have the option of a drive, and the opponent has to cover both long and short.

SEE PRACTICES FOR CROSS COURT DROPS ON PAGE 83-84

Cross-court drop
The cross-court drop is struck further in the front than the straight drop.

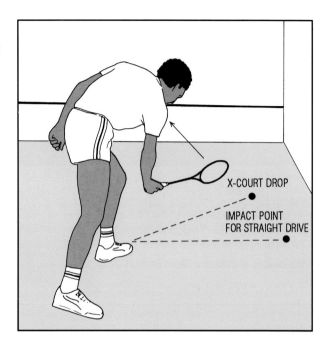

X-COURT DROP

IMPACT POINT
FOR STRAIGHT DRIVE

Volley drops

Having hit the ball to length, and thus forced an opponent into a defensive position at the back of the court, the astute player will be hunting the ball in an attempt to play it to the front of the court as early as possible to produce a winner, or at least to make the opponent run. The volley drop is just such a shot and is arguably the most important attacking shot in the game.

Note: Like the long drop, the volley drop is often considered too advanced for beginners, but again, with lots of work preceding on the basic racket-control exercises, it is not unrealistic for them to have a try.

Coaching points

1. Keep the wrist firm, take the racket-head back as early as possible, keeping the backswing as short as possible.
2. Try to line up the shoulders with the direction of aim.

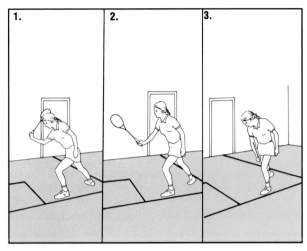

1. **2.** **3.**

Volley drops
Preparation for the forehand,
(top 1) involves cocking the
wrist and a short take-back,
and for the backhand
(bottom 1) involves taking the
racket-head up and getting
the shoulders in line with the
direction of aim. At the point
of impact (2) the wrist is
cocked/racket-head up and
the weight is forwards on to
the front foot with the racket-
face open. In the follow-
through (3) the wrist is still
cocked so the racket-head
stays up as the racket goes
through the ball in the
direction of the aim.

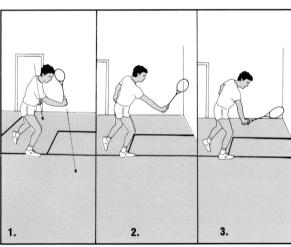

1. **2.** **3.**

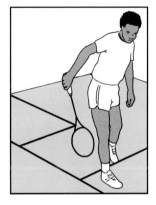

**Faulty follow-through -
Backhand volley drop**
It is very common on the
backhand volley drop for the
racket-head to drop in the
follow-through leading to a loss
of control. Avoid this by
keeping the wrist cocked.

3. Step forwards so the body weight goes into the shot. (This is one of the most crucial factors in playing any short shot.)

4. With the wrist firm, the racket-head up and the racket-face open, stroke through and slightly downwards, with a slow blocking action (similar to tennis volley), keeping the shoulders still throughout.

5. Aim to hit two walls; the ball first hitting the front- wall, then low on the side-wall or landing in the nick.

6. Keeping the racket-head up throughout, strike the ball firmly but not hard, and follow through in the direction of aim.

7. If the ball is close to the side-wall so there is no angle to go for the nick, aim to play an even slower stroke with the racket-face slightly more open in order to take the pace off the ball. This will ensure that it stays short, whilst still achieving a safe height.

Note: This is difficult, and will be beyond all but the most gifted beginners (indeed, many supposedly 'good players' have little or no mastery of this skill), but I think it is important to make the point, if only for future reference.

Hints and tips

• Stress the similarity to tennis to those with experience of that game.

• Control is easier if the elbow is kept into the side as far as possible.

• Get players to think of stroking from the shoulder, keeping the arm still as a single 'unit', to eliminate the unnecessary movement (and thus error).

• Keep the wrist still on the full-stretch volley drops, when the arm may have to be straight.

• As always, encourage pupils to think fingernails/knuckles through the ball to the target point.

• Stress accuracy before power.

Demonstration

With pupils on the side-wall near the short line, demonstrate the two-wall volley drop. Repeat with them positioned behind the racket, and then show them the 'pace-off' shot close to the side-wall, with the pupils standing at the back of the court.

Fault diagnosis

Pupil's problem	Likely cause	Coach's advice
Ball comes back too far down court	• Racket-head moving too fast • Not hitting two walls	• Cock/lock wrist; slow and shorten swing • Line up feet/shoulders
Ball hitting tin too often	• No margin for error • Poor follow-through, probably with racket-head dropping at impact	• Aim higher (but slow) • Keep wrist cocked/racket-head up throughout, and think of fingernails/knuckles through ball
Inconsistent direction	• Shoulder rotation	• Keep everything still except for arm moving from the shoulder
Poor control on overhead shot	• Stance too open • Wrist flappy	• Turn to line up the shoulders, especially on FH • Keep wrist firm

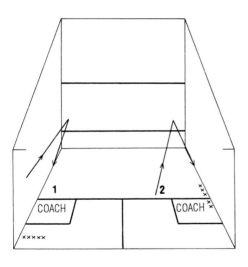

Demonstrating the volley drop

The pace-off volley drop, with the ball 'tight' to the side-wall, should be demonstrated with the pupils watching from behind (1). The two-wall volley drop should be demonstrated with the pupils watching from the side (2).

Lobs

The lob is a high, slow shot which gives the striker time to recover to the 'T', and at the same time make the opponent play a difficult volley or face moving right to the back of the court. It can be played straight or cross-court, from the front or back of the court and is very useful for slowing down the attacking opponent. Whilst it is seen essentially as a defensive shot, its attacking potential should not be underrated.

Coaching points

1. Bend the knees to get under the ball.
2. Begin the stroke early, so the racket can travel slowly.
3. Aim to hit the ball out in front of the leading foot (see note on footwork below) when the racket will be on the way upwards.
4. Stroke very slowly up through the ball with the wrist firm and the racket-face almost completely open, aiming as high as possible on the front wall.
5. Follow through vertically, keeping the head still.
6. The cross-court lob should be taken even further in front, and directed just like the serve to hit the opposite side-wall around the back of the service box.

Note: Footwork - Since it is always easier to reach out with the right foot for a right-handed player (the body is not then twisted), most lobs will be played off the right foot on both sides when stretched. Given time, however, it makes sense to get the left foot across to the forehand lob as the resulting position gives a greater choice of shot, and much better control on the straight length shots. So encourage pupils to get the left foot across to the forehand, and then let them try off the right.

In either case, a long last stride helps the player to stop and get down to the ball.

Hints and tips

The key to good lobbing is getting the ball to strike the front-wall high, so let beginners bounce the ball and aim for the out-of-court line, using an action-replay-speed stroke.

• Emphasize the difference in height, but similarity in speed, of the drop and lob. Keep reminding them that height equals time.
• Stress the importance of stopping/putting the brakes on before attempting to play the stroke.
• Try using a stopwatch to time how long the ball is in the air - anyone who can join the two-second club is doing pretty well!

Demonstration

Just as for the straight drop, for the front court lob or the lob from the back of the court, pupils have to be off-court to get a satisfactory view.

Lob - Forehand cross-court

The point of impact (1) is well out in front of the front foot with the racket-face very open and the racket-head travelling upwards. The follow-through (2) is upwards with the head staying still.

Fault diagnosis

Pupil's problem	Likely cause	Coach's advice
No height (time) on lob	• Ball striking the front-wall too low	• Bend knees more to get under the ball and really open racket-face
Ball hitting the roof	• Racket-head moving too fast	• Keep wrist firm, and swing as slowly as possible
Ball hitting back-wall without bouncing	• Being hit too hard and too low on front-wall	• Make it slow and high and emphasize the need to stay with the ball, and to maintain the same speed of swing throughout
Outcome just inconsistent	• Too many moving parts	• Try to keep the body and head still as racket swings through

SEE PRACTICES FOR LOBS ON PAGES 84-85

Concentration

Although not a specific racket-skill, but a general ability to focus attention on the task in hand, concentration is vital to squash, to minimize the number of unforced errors. This mental skill can be worked upon through any practices which require a certain number of successful shots rather than working for a fixed time.

Movement

Movement becomes important as soon as a player can strike the ball fairly consistently in a static position. Good footwork has to be learned and practised just like a basic racket-skill. Players should practise movement whenever they are given a specific routine to do. No position of the feet is strictly right or wrong: the crucial element is that a player is poised and well-balanced as he hits the ball and can move away smoothly when the shot is played. However, the beginner should be presented with a basic framework of specific positions of the feet for specific shots, which he can later adapt to meet all the demands of matchplay. Coach movement as part of any practice routine. To encourage pupils to take a pride in their movement, have a Best Mover Competition.

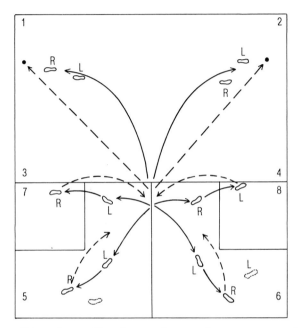

L = Left foot R = Right foot
Ghosting circuit:
1, 2 - Drops (or drives)
3, 4 - Volley lengths
5, 6 - Boasts
7, 8 - Volley drops
Front corners: Move
forwards up the court, then
step across the the ball
(move more across than
forwards on the backhand).
After playing the stroke, push
off the leading foot, to move
backwards to the 'T', along
the same path. Players must
be constantly reminded to
'buy a return ticket'.
Mid-court: Reach the side-
wall in a maximum of two
strides. Try to steady and
play the stroke without
dragging the back foot, and
push back to the 'T' with one
stride if possible. As it is
quicker, try some forehands
off the right foot.
Back corners: Lead into
the back corners with the
right foot. Having played the
shot, push off the right leg to
pivot on the left and facilitate
a fast, economical recovery
to the 'T'. When time permits,
and/or the ball bounces
favourably , the left foot can
be brought back after the
right to the orthodox (dotted)
position.
Note: When ghosting any
shot, in any part of the court,
take the racket back on the
way to the ball; there is then
much more time to really
steady before playing the
stroke. Also players should
develop the habit of looking
'at the ball' as they recover to
the 'T'.

Ghosting - Getting to know the way round the court

Invented by Jonah Barrington and borrowed by countless coaches and players ever since, it is simply the process of moving around the court without the ball but playing strokes as realistically as possible. I am convinced that it is by far the best way to establish the essential patterns of movement, but it isn't always popular with pupils, so approach the practice with humour.

Begin with a basic ghosting circuit, in which players learn to move to and from the six most important points of the court: the four corners, and either end of the short-line. Start by getting pupils to float ghosts, moving slowly and smoothly around the court, taking the minimum number of strides possible. (NB It is fine to have four players doing this simultaneously and it can work with up to six.) Point out that two longer strides are quicker than four shorter, faster ones, as well as being more energy-efficient.

Movement
1. Backhand drive: Aim to move to one side of the ball at the front of the court, then step across to play it.
2. Backhand volley: Try not to drag the back foot. Stretch out on to - and push back off - the right foot.
3. Forehand when stretched: Lead with the right foot to both forehands and backhands in the back corners.
4. Forehand when time: If time permits, the left foot can be brought across in order to play in the orthodox position.

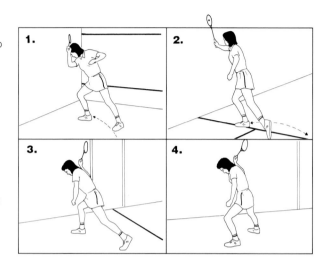

Movement Problems

1. Front corners

When moving to the front of the court, players tend to run straight at the ball and not turn enough to be able to play the shot down the wall with any conviction. They must be reminded to aim at one side of the ball and then step across to play the shot. It can also be pointed out that in this position it is still possible to play a cross-court shot merely by taking the ball a little earlier, but the straight shot from a stance which is too open is much more difficult, especially on the backhand side. In addition, beginners often forget to move backwards on the return to the 'T' and neglect to watch the ball as they do so.

2. Midcourt

The crucial shot here is the volley. There is often a tendency to drag the back foot after playing the shot, and this results in one or more extra strides being taken to return to the 'T'. Pupils should be reminded to stretch out on to, and push back off the leading foot, dragging the back foot as little as possible.

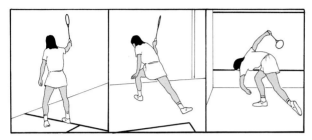

3. Back corners

As in front corners players tend to run at the ball, getting into the corner with it, and then have to try to play a shot off their shins. They have to be reminded that it is usually much easier to step back, so they will play the ball out of the back corners much better if they think of keeping out of the serving box 'alley' (marked by a continutaion of the service box line) until they can see exactly where the ball is going.

Once conditioned to get the left foot across to a forehand corner with the left foot leading - this not only makes the stroke difficult (having to hit across the left leg), but renders the recovery to the 'T' very laborious. On the backhand side, this is not a problem, because the shoulder hitting the ball is the one nearest to the 'T' so there is not so far to turn and recovery is relatively easy. For these reasons players should practise stretching back on to the right foot on both sides of the court. However, if time permits/ the player is not stretched, the left foot can be brought back after the right, and placed so the shot is played with the feet ion the orthodox position.

4. Over-running the ball

Because they are not yet strong in the upper leg, and to make matters worse, have probably grown considerably in height, children are inclined not to be able to stop when they reach the ball.This results in uncontrolled shots, and an inability to recover to the 'T' afterwards. It is especially bad when moving fast to the front corners, and this movement particularly should be practised by ghosting, trying to take a longer last stride, in order to apply the brakes. Associated with the leg problem is a general collapse led by the head going down towards the floor after the shot has been played; this is especially so on the backhand side at the front.

Incorrect movement
Far left: Backhand volley
If the shoulders swing round and the left foot is dragged, at least one extra stride is necessary to recover to the 'T'.
Centre: Forehand back corner
If the left foot leads into the forehand back corner, the shot is difficult and the recovery to the 'T' laborious because there is so far to turn.
Left: Front backhand corner
The unlikely position illustrated is quite common in junior players: unable to stop properly, the back foot begins to be dragged through, the head goes down and the shoulders swing whilst the follow-through becomes inverted. Recovery to the 'T' is tricky from here.

Tactics

Once the battle to teach the beginners how to hit the ball shows some signs of being won, it is time to guide them in tactical thinking. All too often the beginner will play the easy shot rather than the best one, and even when he does select the right shot, it probably won't go where he meant it to. So as a coach, don't expect the manifestations of your brilliant tactical teaching to be over evident too soon!

Improving tactical play

Tactics involve selecting the correct shot to play and this ability comes about through a combination of practical experience and coach's advice. Players learn gradually by 'trial and error', but tactics can be coached during a practice game by the coach starting on court, pointing out missed opportunities and errors while they are still fresh in the player's mind.

The coach can also engage his players in conditioned games which, with their particular rules, force the participants to concentrate on tactical considerations such as maintaining good length or taking the ball early, for example.

Some basic tactical points

- If in doubt , hit the ball STRAIGHT (limiting the opponent's choice of shot and providing minimum risk to the striker)
- Try to avoid unforced errors
- Try to dominate the 'T' as it is possible from this position to cover all corners of the court and the opponent is given little space to exploit.
- Hit to good length to 'bury' an opponent in the back corners of the court, where he is least likely to produce a winner and more likely to make an error.
- Try to hit the ball away from your opponent to one of the four corners. The most obvious ploy is to take him to the back and then play short so he has to run. Most errors are made when having to move fast when fatigued.
- Be aware of your opponent's position: look and listen
- Try to volley whenever possible to deprive your opponent of time and save yourself some running.
- Rally your opponent, play safely and let him make the mistake. Remember the two Ps: be Patient but Positive (attack by volleying and taking out the ball early).
- Play with a little margin for error - don't take risks when hard out.
- Never give up. Squash is a game which can be won from apparently impossible positions.
- Try to take a match one shot at a time, one rally at a time, and concentrate really hard when winning.
- Warm up thoroughly and use this time to remind yourself of the basic tactics.
- Use the knock-up to practise your movements and shots and to assess your opponent's strengths and weaknesses.

PRACTICE

Practice

Principles of Practice

Most players would much rather play than practise, so why is it so important? Practice means concentrated work on a shot, free from the pressures of winning the game. Technique can therefore be experimented with and new ideas tried out, which is not possible when winning is a priority. Also a practice routine demands a certain sequence of shots, whereas an ordinary game allows a player to 'opt out' by playing the shot which is easiest, rather than the best. Once established in practice, a new skill can be implemented in the game situation. Practice either solo or with a partner, and preferably both, is not just important but absolutely vital to speedy improvement.

Work at weaknesses

Practice should be geared to improving the weakest areas of a player's game: towards those shots which, because of the likelihood of failure, would be avoided if at all possible in a game.

Make practice relevant

Practice should be a kind of repair job: removing faulty components from the game situation, working to repair/develop/perfect them, and then putting them back in a game to test them out. Consequently it is important to get pupils to practise realistically, adjusting the following variables to resemble match conditions as closely as possible:

• Position from which the shot is played (starting with the easiest)
• Direction of the feed (noting that it is always easiest to stroke through the ball in the line it is travelling)
• Speed of the feed (always begin slowly)
• Target-size, which must be difficult enough to be challenging, but easy enough to ensure some success
• Speed of the ball; use a ball which should resemble match-play characteristics under practice conditions. Thus, it is often better to practise with a white or red-dot ball. The more lively bounce

has the extra advantage of removing the necessity to hit hard all the time, and helps put the emphasis on accuracy before power, a very important principle.

Repetition

Pupils should be encouraged to hit as many of the chosen shots as possible in practice in order to really establish that skill, to 'groove' it. Remember,though, that only perfect practice makes perfect, and pupils must pay attention to detail so that erroneous technique is not 'grooved' in. Stress quality - one good shot is better than ten poor ones.

Make practice interesting

Players often complain that practice is boring, but it need not be. Encourage the use of targets; these can be physical, marked on the floor, or numerical, representing a player's personal best or simply a score to aim for set by the coach. Introduce the idea of 'margin for error', by deducting points for shots which are down or out. Persuade the pupils to keep a squash notebook in which scores can be recorded, and improvement thus measured. Practice is as interesting as you make it!

The importance of progression

For practice to be rewarding and as valuable as possible, players should be encouraged to begin with the easy exercise, and progress steadily to the more difficult. They should not be afraid to go back a stage if the skill begins to break down. The general progressions are as follows:
• Solo practice - static
• Solo practice - with movement
• Pairs-practice routine - cooperative, with a fixed sequence of shots
• Pairs-practice routine - competitive
• Competitive routine/conditioned game - with a choice of shot involved, and therefore a degree of uncertainty.

Ideas for practice
Practice target areas

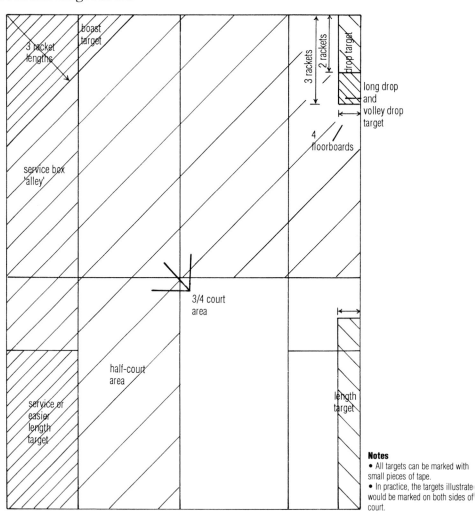

3 racket lengths

boast target

2 rackets

3 rackets

drop target

long drop and volley drop target

4 floorboards

service box 'alley'

3/4 court area

half-court area

length target

service or easier length target

Notes
- All targets can be marked with small pieces of tape.
- In practice, the targets illustrated would be marked on both sides of court.

Notes

1. The practices are aranged under stroke headings so as to correspond with the sections in Chapter 3.

2. All the shots described are straight (i.e. hit down the nearest side-wall) unless otherwise stated.

3. All practices described on one side of the court can be repeated on the other side.

4. In the hand-fed solo practices, it is important that students take the racket back **before** throwing the ball.

5. In the two-ball feed practices, the timing of the feed is critical; coaches should help pupils arrive at a tempo which is demanding but does not over-compromise quality. As a general guide, the second ball should be fed slowly just as the first ball is struck but allowance has to be made for fatigue.

6. There is a thin dividing line between pairs practices and conditioned games. Most practice routines can easily be made competitive by introducing an appropriate scoring system, and a conditioned game can be converted into a competitive practice simply by removing the scoring.

7. To save repeating instructions, the following are standard throughout
Alley - the channel on each side of the court, bounded by an extension of the service-box line to both the front and back-walls, and the side-wall.
1/2-court - where the court is divided into two by an extension of the central/half-court line to the front-wall.
Front-court - the area of the court in front of the short-line.
Length- a ball hit so as to bounce behind the short-line, unless otherwise qualified by a specific target.
3/4-court - the area consisting of the whole of the front half of the court, plus one of the rear quarters (leaving the other rear quarter free for those players who are waiting their turn).
Length target - unless otherwise specified this refers to targets 1 and 2
Drop target - likewise to targets 3 and 4
Volley drop target - the drop targets extended by one racket-length as shown (refer to the coaching court, page 25).

8. Groups - Practices and games listed under this heading are for more than two players. Two-ball feeds can accommodate four players and the 3/4 court games can cope with up to six.

9. Scoring - Unless otherwise stated American scoring is to be used, so every rally counts. Where a rotation is operating, the winner stays on, and the loser drops out. (To avoid one player dominating too much, the coach can stipulate a maximum of, say, five consecutive points.)

Basic Racket Control

• **Chipping** - Standing about a metre from the front-wall, play the ball with a short swing, with the wrist cocked/racket-head up throughout, so the racket-head is above the wrist at all times. **Note:** Must try to keep sideways on.

• **Chipping moving back** - As above but move back down the court slowly, aiming higher on the front-wall until reaching short-line and then move forwards again. Progress to reaching back wall and touching back and front wall with the racket between shots.

• **Volleys at front** - As above, but on the volley. Try alternate fore- and backhands also.

• **Angle volleys** - Stand facing the front corner, about two metres back; play a forehand (FH) volley to hit side-wall/front-wall and then a backhand (BH) volley to hit front-wall/side-wall. How many can be played consecutively?

• **Touch shots** - Place a sheet of A4 card/paper end on to the front-wall against the side-wall. Standing sideways on to the corner, stroke the ball as gently/slowly as possible, trying to land it on the card.

Drives

Solo

• **Driving boasts** - Standing just in front of the 'T', turn towards the side-wall and drive the ball hard and fairly high, as if boasting; turn to follow path of ball and take racket back for same stroke onto opposite side-wall i.e. alternate FH and BH.

• **Service-box shots** - Aim to play medium-pace drives to bounce in the service box. Progress to consecutive shots to box.

• **Target drives** - Rally to the back of court aiming for the length target. How many in twenty goes, or two minutes?

• **Back-wall drives** - Aim to slightly overhit drives and try to take ball after back-wall to get it back to length.

Pairs

• **Cooperative rally** - Maximum number of consecutive shots bouncing in half-court/back-half court/alley/length alley.

• **Boast drive** - One player boasts alternate sides; the other drives alternately FH and BH. How many without a mistake? Both players should try to get to the 'T' between shots.

• **Boast/drive cross-court** - Rally, then progress to movement to 'T' between shots.

• **Drive/drive/boast** - Rally first, then progress to competing.

• **Boast/drive** - Straight or cross-court.

Groups

• **Two-ball feed** - One player driving straight, one player each side feeding straight with ball bouncing just in front of short-line. How many in five minutes? Progress to:

• **Both feeds short**

• **Both feeds longer**, to behind short-line

• **One feed short**, the other long.

• **Three-quarter court rallies or games** - Fixed rally of, say, boast/cross-court drive/straight drive etc or a game within the restricted area, bonus points for hitting straight length target.

Coach feed

• **From the back corner**, with one player on the 'T' and the rest of the group queued up in the opposite back corner. Straight feed for a straight drive, after which the player can move to the opposite front corner to 'ghost' a BH drop before joining the back of the queue. Group rotates. Count targets hit.

• Same feeding position, but each player has two shots each time eg short feed/straight drive, followed by boast feed/cross- court drive etc.

Conditioned games

• **Half court** - Any shot can be used, providing the ball bounces on correct side of court. Add interest by scoring bonus points for any length-targets hit (two players each side).

• **Alley game** - As above, but the ball must bounce within the service-box alley.

Note: When players are competent enough to play the alley game without straying too far, a fifth player can be incorporated, waiting against the door, and taking the place of the first player to lose the rally etc. This ensures a mix of players and gives practice on both sides. It can be applied to any Alley Game.

• **All-length game** - Ball must bounce behind short-line or the point is lost. Score bonus points for length targets (two players only).

Volleys

Solo

• **Quarter-court volleys** - Standing half way between the short line and front-wall, play a volley on to front-wall. Maximum number without a mistake.

• **Short-line volleys** - As above, but standing behind short-line.

• **Moving volleys** - Starting at front, move back down court to short-line, volleying all the time. Move up to front-wall again, and try to touch the wall with the racket between the shots. (Very useful for getting players to stroke slowly)

•**'10's' volleys** - Starting at front, play ten consecutive volleys, move back one step and play ten more etc.

Pairs

• **Cross-court volleys** - One player each side; volley cross court to each other.

• **Target-length volleys** - One player feeds straight from behind, for partner to volley straight for target. Swap over, and compete as a pair (so the quality of the feed as well as the volley is crucial).

• **Slow control volleys** - Players facing each other across the court, volleying to maximum rally (a very useful practice for developing control, but slow stroke must be emphasized, and players need to be fairly competent).

Groups

• **Two-ball feed** - Straight feeds /straight volleys to length-targets. Progress to straight or cross-court feed/straight or cross-court volley to match.

• **Three-quarter court rally or game** - Anywhere in prescribed area, with one point per rally played.

Coach feed

• Feeding from the back, as for Drives group practice.

• As above, but cross-court feed/cross-court volley.

• Same rotation of group, but two shots each: one straight, one cross-court.

• As above, but one drive and one volley.

Conditioned games

• **Alley game** - with American scoring plus one point per volley.

• **Cross-court volley game** - Aiming to land the ball in the opposite back corner to score a point.

• **One point per volley game** - using the whole court. (Remind players to adjust their score every time they hit a volley, not to try to remember at the end of a long rally!)

• **Defend the back-wall game** - A player loses the point if he leaves his opponent's shot to bounce and hit the back-wall.

Service and service return

Solo Service

• **Basic height/width serve** - Ball must hit the opposite side-wall and bounce into the alley behind the service box. Have, say, ten goes, and work out the percentage success (this can be done for any practice, and really brings home to players the importance of consistency).

• **Variations** - Once the basic serve is reliable, try variations for surprise like hard and low for the nick; straight at the opponent; or sharper angles off the side-wall.

Return

• **Hand-feed/volley** - Facing side-wall in normal position, throw ball gently on to side-wall just in front of leading foot (racket back before throwing). Wait for the ball to come off wall, and volley high and straight, aiming to land it in the length-target. Work out percentage success again.

Pairs

• **Hand-feed/return** - One player throws the ball across the diagonal of service-box on to side-wall, and steps back to the middle line of court (to be safe from the return struck too early). Receiver plays straight volley return, aiming for the length-target. So many goes; count targets; swap over.

• **Two-shot rally/game** - One player serves, say ten times, whilst other player returns, aiming for length-target. Swap and repeat as many times as needed! Score on targets hit.

Groups

• **Server/jumpers** - One player serves, with the rest of group on short-line jumping trying to intercept. Ten goes and swap; score one point for landing ball in alley, five points if it hits the side-wall first.

• **Three- quarter court game** - Must volley the service return to land in half-court/alley/alley behind short-line, as appropriate.
Coach feed
Coach serves - Pupils rotate, trying to return serve to length target. (Coaches should be careful not to 'hog' the court-time, but with that reservation, pupils do love to try to beat the coach, who must be prepared to play nine brilliant shots without applause, but suffer great derision for his one error!)

Conditioned games
Ordinary game - Must volley the service return with serves played for height and width. Further conditions can cover the direction of the return.

Boast

Solo
• Hand feed to bounce ball on back corner of service-box then boast, trying to land ball in target triangle. (See page 72)
Note: Target can be marked with tape, or with a spare racket or cover and should be adjusted to suit ability/ambition.
• **Back-corner hand feed** - Facing back corner, throw ball back-wall, side-wall, boast to target. Progress to the side wall/back-wall feed, or simply lower feeds; then feed from nearer to 'T', moving back to the corner for the boast.

Pairs
• **Drive/boast routine** - As for pairs practice for drives.
• **Drive straight or cross-court/boast** - As for pairs practice for drives.
• **Length/length/boast** - Two drives or volleys to length, followed by the boast. Score American plus target points.

Groups
• **Two boasting/one driving** - Boasters trying to prevent driver hitting targets. So many goes, and rotate.
• **Three-quarter court rally** - Boast/cross-court Drive/straight. Length/boast etc.
• **Three-quarter court game** - Limited shots. Straight drive or boast only in back corner and cross-court. Drive from front off boast.

Coach Feed
• Coach feeds cross-court from front corner for group to boast in rotation.
• As above, but player hits straight length (drive or volley) off cross-court and then boasts his own shot. Targets can be counted for both lengths and boasts.

Conditioned games

• **Drive/Boast game** - Serve as normal, returning straight to length. Server boasts, receiver drives. American scoring; winner serves. (Serve with a boast if service return is too difficult.)
Note: In all conditioned games, make sure that the winner of each rally has the more difficult condition for the next, to help prevent it becoming unfair. In the above game, the winner serves, and therefore has to boast, which is the more difficult shot with which to win the rally.
• **Alleys game** - Game where all shots must be straight ie bounce in the alley- unless the boast is used to swap sides; no boasting off a boast (much more valuable to practise straightening). Progress to two-wall boasts only - lose point if boast hits opposite side-wall without bouncing ('nicks' and very near misses count as two-wall).

Volley boast
Solo
• Play some quarter-court volleys but after say five shots, turn and play the volley boast. Chip back on other side of the court and volley again for five, the volley boast etc. Progress to moving deeper in the court.
Pairs
• **Drive/volley boast routine** - As for boast/drive , but the boaster tries volley boast, whilst the driver tries to stop him by keeping it 'tight' to side-wall.

Straightening
Solo
• Face the side-wall near where it joins the back-wall, with enough room to swing the racket with wrist cocked. Throw the

ball to the back-wall/side-wall and try to hit ball high and straight to come back to the length-target. Work out percentage success. Progress to:
1. Feed which stays closer to back-wall
2. Side-wall/back-wall feed
3. Feed from nearer to the 'T', moving back to play shot.
Note: The first two can be played with a shortened grip
• As for solo back-wall drives, but progress to higher, slower drives which don't come so far off the back-wall.

Pairs/Conditioned Games
• **All-length alley or half-court game** - Score target points for good length, and double points for anything 'straightened' to target after the back wall. (Choose a suitable target: the back half of the alley is plenty challenging enough to start with, and the practice is only for the more competent anyway.)
• All-length game using the whole court, but with no boasts.

Groups
• **Two-ball feed** - One player straightening to target off hand-feeds into back corners of back-wall, side-wall (feeders standing near back-wall, close to the half-court line). Progress to one feeding as described, with the other feeding shorter for an ordinary drive (the movement back to the ball makes it much more difficult).

Drop shots

Solo
• Hand feed into front corner, front-wall/side-wall, from about a metre away; line up feet/shoulders in direction of aim, and play drop to target (four floorboards wide by one racket length). Progress to feeding from further away.
• **Three-wall boast feed** - Feed high, medium-paced boast from just in front of the 'T', turn and play straight. Drop to target (four floor-boards wide x two racket-lengths) ie FH boast, BH drop and vice versa.
• **Two-wall boast feed** - Standing just a little further forwards, repeat above practice but feeding a slow, low boast which falls well short of the second side-wall.

• **Cross-court drop** - As above, or utilizing a straight feed, but aiming for the target on the far side of court.

Pairs

• **Boast/drop lob** - One player boasts, the other player plays a straight drop to target (two racket-lengths) and then lobs his own shot straight. How many targets in certain number of goes?

• **Boast/drop/counter-drop/lob** - First player boasts, second player plays straight drop, first player moves forward and plays a straight counter-drop (a drop off a drop). The second player then plays a straight lob, the first player responds with a boast on the other side, and the sequence is repeated.

Note: This practice is also a very good movement exercise, but it is difficult for beginners, so begin by making it cooperative. Progress to trying for winners ; play to a winning drop and swap over, or continue for ,say, ten drops.

• **Boast/drop/length/boast** - First player boasts, second player drops straight, first player moves forwards and hits straight length shot, second player moves to back and boasts etc. Again a demanding practice, so make it cooperative first and then make it competitive.

Groups

• **Two-ball feed** - One player playing all straight drops off a straight feed on alternate sides (racket or hand feed), or off a hand feed front-wall/side-wall from near the middle of the front-wall. Count targets. Progress to one deeper feed for a drive or volley, with a drop feed on the other side, so player has to move.

• **Short-alley game** - Two players each side, play out point just in front half of the alley; winner serves from front of alley, and serve may not be a winner.

Note: Safety - keep it safe by outlawing anything hit hard. (This exercise is surprisingly popular and valuable; it can accommodate up to six players, with the losers of each rally dropping out.)

• **Front-court game** - Boast to serve and play out the rally just in front half-court. Progress to server plays straight drops only.

• **Cross-court drops** - As above, but nothing straight. All boasts and cross-court drops.

Coach feed

• Coach feeds a boast from one back corner; one pupil on 'T' with rest of group waiting behind in other back corner. First player

---

Group coach feed practice 'Kill the coach'

Coach boasts for first player to play a straight drop; coach moves up to play counter-drop and pupil plays a lob (straight or cross-court, or either); coach goes back to boast etc, and rally continues to an error from pupil, or submission of the coach!

moves forwards to play straight drop (and moves out of way), second player moves in for cross-court lob and returns to 'T', before moving forwards again to play straight drop off coach's next boast etc.

• Coach feeds straight from back corner for first player to play straight length then boasts the same for players to play the drop etc. Court targets, or let player carry on until he makes a mistake.

Conditioned games

• **Boast/drop/length game** - As for pairs boast/drop/length/boast practice, but with proper serve and American scoring.

• Normal game but must drop off a boast.

Long drops
Solo

•**'T' angle feed** - From 'T', feed with a BH stroke into FH front corner to hit front-wall/side-wall, and return for FH long drop to be played from just in front of short-line, aiming for target (three racket-lengths initially).

Note: Using a BH feed for a FH shot helps the fluency of the stroke, because the follow through after the feed leaves the racket ready for the shot being practised.

Progress to faster and/or deeper feeds

• **Straight feed** - Still playing drop from short-line, but using a straight feed, bouncing closer to side-wall with the same target.

• **Back corner drop** - Facing back corner, hand feed back-wall/side-wall and play long drop for target. Progress to racket-feed by driving to back.

• **Cross-court** - As for practices above but aiming for target on other side of court.

Pairs

• **Service-box feed** - One player feeding from front trying to land ball in service box; the other player hitting long drops to target. Count targets hit after, say, 20 feeds to service box. (Whenever it is possible, give the feeder something to really aim for). This also works well as a competition between pairs, with each player feeding for, say, five minutes.

• As above, but using both sides of court, with feeder aiming for either service box.

Groups
• **Three-quarter court game** - Must play a long drop from the back quarter of court, except for the service return. Shots can be played long or short off anything in front half of court.
Coach feed
• Coach feeding from front to behind short-line with the group rotating to play long drop straight. Since errors are more likely than winners, give each player ten lives and they then lose a life for each error - last one left alive wins!

Conditioned games
• **Long versus short alley game** - Server has to hit everything to front half of the court; receiver all to back half. (Or, to concentrate the practice, one player hits all short for five minutes, then swap).
• **Long versus short game** - As above, but using the whole court.

Volley drops
Solo
• **Hand feed** - Standing near front corner, throw ball front-wall, side-wall and play the volley drop to target (one racket-length).
Progress by feeding from further back
• **Angle feed** - Standing just in front of 'T', feed a BH into the FH front corner to hit front-wall/side-wall; play volley drop to target (start with three racket-lengths). Progress by feeding from deeper, and/or increasing the speed of the feed, then reduce target to two racket lengths.
• **Straight feed** - Feed straight down side-wall, play volley drop trying to keep it 'tight' to side-wall.
Progress by feeding deeper and/or faster, and then reduce target to two racket lengths

Pairs
• **Tennis volleys** - Facing partner across the court, volley slowly to each other, FH to FH or vice versa.
• **Cooperative rally** - One player at the front, feeding ball straight to reach short-line at about shoulder height, for partner to play volley drop to target (three racket -lengths to start with).

Groups
• **Three-quarter court game** - One point per volley, but all volleys must be hit to front half of the court.

Coach feed
• From front court for group to rotate, playing the volley drop around the short-line (moving from 'T', and then backwards after playing it). Count targets, or give lives.
• Cross-court for group to rotate (queued in the corner behind first player), each playing a volley drop straight, and following it in to play ball back to coach with a cross-court drop or boast.

Conditioned games
• **Long versus short alley game** - As described for long drop practice
• **Long versus short game** - Using the whole court server all short (so he can serve, and move across to 'hunt' the volley drop).

Lobs

Solo
• Hand feed at front of court, get under ball, and aim for out of court line on front-wall. Aim really high, even if ball hits roof and gradually aim a little lower/stroke a little slower, so ball bounces before back-wall.

Pairs
• **Straight lob** - One player feeds short and straight, from just behind short-line. The other player lobs straight and the feeder jumps (without moving back) to try to touch the ball with his racket.Count the number of successful lobs.
• **Cross-court lob** - As above, feeder does so with a boast (or hand feed into corner if necessary).
• **Boast/lob** - Either straight or cross-court. Lobs can be incorporated into a continuous rally; swap over after each winning lob.
• **Boast/cross-court lob/straight length/boast** - This sequence means considerable running, so it is difficult; begin by just trying to maintain the routine, with lobs and straight lengths having to bounce in the back quarter of court. Progress to make it competitive with straight lengths having to be in the alley.

Groups
• As for first two pairs practices above, but with multiple jumpers.

It can be organized on team lines, with each member of one team taking his turn to feed ten boasts for his team mates to lob. Points are scored for beating the jumpers. Teams swap over.

• **Three-quarter game** - Server all to front half of the court, the receiver all to the back half.

• **Two-ball feed** - Introducing more movement into the practice, the feeders can again be jumpers. Progress to a combination of, say, volley on one side, lob on the other.

Coach feed

• Coach feeds boast or cross-court volley from the back corner and group is queued up as usual. First player plays cross-court lob, with next player trying to intercept it on the volley that player then plays the next lob. Score it as a 'black mark' for the lobber if he hits it out or his lob is volleyed to length - fewest black marks wins.

Conditioned games

• **Long versus short alley game** - As described in practice for long drops.

• **Long versus short all-court game** - Server playing all to front half; receiver all to the back.

• **'Cut-line' game** - One player hitting anywhere, the other playing all above the cut-line. Five minutes and swap, or server all above cut-line.

• **Angle volleys** - Described in basic racket control practices. As players get better, they are able to do high repetitions of this practice, which demands good concentration. (There is also an arm-strengthening benefit).

• **Patience rally** - Player begins at the front on FH side, and chips back until he hits the ball into the length-target (this can be the alley behind the service-box or the narrow target, depending upon standard). He then boasts as soon as he can, moves forwards to play a drop on the BH side, and repeats the practice down that wall, boasting to get onto the FH side again. This time he must hit two shots into the target before boasting, and the next time three etc. Time how long to complete ten sequences.

Tactical factors

As players improve and develop a basic ability to hit a particular shot with some success, the coach can begin to encourage his pupils to use the various skills more effectively/tactically. The final section of Chapter 3 highlighted certain tactical advice; the following notes are suggestions of how that advice can be applied through the appropriate conditioned game:

• **Hitting good length** - One player hitting all to length, the other hitting anywhere he likes, but he is not allowed to volley (except for the service return), so the effectiveness of the length shot can be seen. Server all length, or one game and swap

• **Good width - Avoiding the 'T' area.** Either player wins the point if he can play the ball with one foot still on the 'T'

• **Hunting the volley** - One point per volley game

• **Avoiding unforced errors** - Play a normal game, but any unforced error is immediately punished by that player doing ten squat thrusts

• **Hitting the ball away from the opponent**- three-quarter court game, with one player hitting everything to the back corner, whilst the other one tries to hit it away from him

• **Using height** - See conditioned cut-line game for lobs.

Keeping it tight to the side-wall

• **Alley rally** - Solo practice, moving up and down the alley, trying to keep the ball close to the side-wall

• **One all - straight game** - One player hitting everything straight, the other anywhere. Server all straight, or one game and swap.

• **Taking it early** - Begin the alley rally, described above, from the back of the alley, and move forwards taking the ball at the top of the bounce. Progress to taking it on the rise

• **Accuracy before power** - Play a normal game, but score bonus points for any shot bouncing in one of the four targets shown in the illustration on page 72.

Footnote to practices
Although improvement on the basic racket control exercises should be fairly noticeable to both coach and players, don't expect miracles with the routines and conditioned games; many of those described are very demanding. Wiith suitable encouragement and help, however, beginners will soon rise to the challenge. Remember success with a routine may initially be simply the completion of a sequence, even though the shots may be scrappy, and with the first attempts at a conditioned game, they will be doing well if they can just abide by the rules. Persevere and improvement will gradually be made.

FITNESS TRAINING

Fitness Training

It is common knowledge that squash is one of the most physically demanding of activities. Therefore, so the argument goes, fitness training is the key to success. This is not the case with beginners, young children especially. Remember, the beginner is inefficient in his efforts and will expend more energy than he needs, even when he is just trying to play so he will get fitter anyway. Fitness training becomes crucial when a player is losing primarily because he is not fit enough, and consequently is very seldom a priority for a beginner, who loses because he is inconsistent in his skills or tactically naive.

There is sometimes confusion, particularly amongst beginners, between practice and training. Practice is aimed at perfecting the racket, tactical and movement skills, whilst training is concerned purely with the physical condition of the body. Happily, it is often possible to combine the two, since a practice routine/conditioned game which involves lots of running is also developing physical fitness specific to squash. Although the emphasis with beginners must be on skills, the coach should understand the principles of fitness training.

Squash fitness can be broken down into:

• **Cardio-vascular or cardio-respiratory fitness,** which refers to the efficiency of the heart and lungs to take in and distribute oxygen to the working muscles. Training is by aerobic exercise where sufficient oxygen is present to meet the energy demands of the activity. Suitable exercises to assist this are running, skipping, cycling and swimming.

• **Local muscle endurance,** which refers to the ability of the muscles to keep working under prolonged and varied work loads. This requires both aerobic and anaerobic training. Anaerobic exercise is where intense work loads render the body incapable of providing sufficient oxygen, and production of energy by a different physiological pathway results in an oxygen debt and a build up of lactic acid. When this build up reaches a certain level, the work rate falls and the exercise becomes aerobic, the oxygen debt being gradually repaid. Suitable exercises include circuit training, ghosting, the playing of continuous rally games and multi-gym work.

• **Speed,** which is the ability to think, react and move fast. This can be improved by training, utilizing movements requiring maximum effort for very short periods, and suitable exercises include fast ghosting and short sprints.

• **Strength,** which is often not a limiting factor, although players must be able to grip the racket firmly. Children are clearly physically weak, but it is not safe for them to undertake strength training, save for actually playing the game. Pure strength-training is achieved in multi-gym work.

• **Agility** which is the ability to twist, turn, move fast and still maintain balance. This is best practised on the court, with games and routines, although coordination can be improved by circuit-type exercises and balance tests (try getting children to stand on one leg with their eyes closed!)

• **Flexibility,** which is the ability to stretch for the ball and is dependent on the range of movement of the joints and the length of the muscles. It can be improved by stretching exercises, and this is one of the areas very suitable for the training of beginners.

• **Percentage body fat** is a factor in the work and stress that exercise puts on the joints. The lower the percentage the better for squash players. Some pre-adolescent children are chubby before they lose it as they stretch out with growth; over-weight adults need to look carefully at their diet, for exercise alone is seldom the way to lose excess body fat.

It should be noted that the coach who draws up his sessions carefully, with the aim of improving skill through maximum activity, will almost inevitably be training his pupils at the same time as they work with the racket.

Ideas for Training Beginners

The following exercises are safe and of value to beginners, including children, and are specifically for fitness. One of their main virtues is that they are suitable for occupying players profitably while they are waiting off-court in a squad situation.

Head and neck *
Look right; look left; look up/back and down; then slowly roll the head starting with one ear on the shoulder, then the chin on the chest, the other ear on the other shoulder and round. Do this exercise in both directions.

Shoulder Rolls *
Roll the shoulders gently backwards, forwards then backwards again, making as big a circle as possible.

Arm circles *
With thumbs interlocked, stretch the arms back without bending the elbows and hold. Part the hands and circle the arms backwards very slowly. Repeat in the opposite direction.

Shoulders
With fingers interlocked behind you and without leaning forwards, lift the hands backwards as high as possible, keeping the elbows straight.

Arms/Shoulders (1)
Reach down the back with one hand, pulling the elbow back gently with the other hand. Then try reaching down the back with one hand and up behind the back with the other - try to link fingers.

Fore-arm (2)
With elbow slightly bent, fist lightly clenched and wrist dropped, gently pull the knuckles in towards the body with the other hand. Feel the stretch up the forearm to the elbow.
• With arm outstretched, palm upwards, gently pull the fingers down and back.

Back - Side-bends (3)
Without reaching forwards or bending the knee, reach down the side of the leg as far as possible.

Back - Back-arches (4)
With arms stretched above the head,

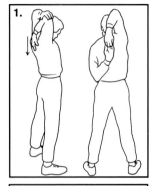

bend backwards, reaching and looking as low as possible.

Lower back - Hip-circles *
With feet about shoulder-width apart, make as large a circle as possible with the hips. Keep the shoulders still.

Quadriceps
Standing on one leg, bend the other leg and pull the foot up towards the buttock, trying to keep the shoulders back.

Hip Adductors - Side-splits (5)
With the front foot pointing away, and the back foot at right angles to it,

bend the front knee, while keeping the weight over the straight back leg.

Hip-flexors - Tight-rope (6)
With both feet pointing forwards, bend the front knee while keeping the back leg straight and the shoulders pulled back.

Hip flexor/hamstring/groin - Splits
Starting with both feet pointing in the same direction, gently ease them as far apart as possible while trying to keep the legs straight. Use the hands for support if necessary.

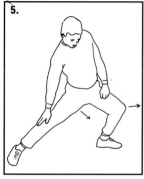

5.

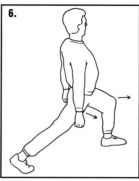

6.

7.

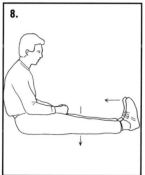

8.

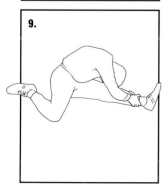

9.

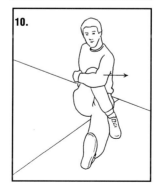

10.

Adductor/groin - Knees to floor
In sitting position, put the soles of the feet together, press the knees down as near to the floor as possible and gently lean forwards.

Hamstring/Calf - Touching toes (7)
Sitting with the legs outstretched, lean forwards and reach to grasp toes if possible, or as far as comfortable and hold.

Quadriceps/patella - Knee locks (8)
Not a stretch, but a worthwhile strengthening exercise. Sitting with legs straight, press the back of the knees to the floor while pulling the toes up towards you. The heels should lift off the floor. Hold.

Hamstring/groin - Hurdles (9)
With one leg outstretched and the other out to the side at right angles with the knee bent, put both hands on the bent knee and circle round to touch the out-stretched leg or foot and hold.

Adductors - Nose to floor
With feet as wide apart as possible, and the legs straight, reach forwards keeping the back as straight as possible.

Buttocks (10)
With one leg outstretched, put the outside of the other foot against the outside of the outstretched thigh, and pull in the bent knee with the opposite elbow. Feel the stretch in the buttock of the bent leg.

Trunk (11, see overleaf)
From the above position, put the back of the elbow on the other side of the knee and push towards the straight leg, turning the head to look behind. Feel the stretch across the middle-back.

Hip/groin (12, see overleaf) *
Using the wall for support, stand on the

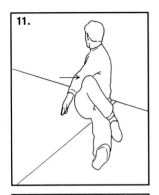

11.

12.

leg nearest the wall and lift the knee of the other leg as high as possible. Take it out to the side to the limit and lower it again. Repeat in the opposite direction.

Calf/Achilles tendon (13)
Leaning against a wall, with one foot forwards and the other back, gently bend the front knee whilst keeping the back heel on the floor.

Ankle (14)
Standing on one leg, rotate the other foot to make as large a circle with the toes as possible.

Lower back/general - Shadow stroking (15) *
Using the hand as a racket, play forehand drives, emphasizing the turn of the trunk from the waist to mobilize the lower back. Repeat on backhand and gradually increase the speed of the stroke and the knee bend.

13.

14.

> **Note**
> * These exercises are not pure stretches, but a combination of a mobilizing exercise and a stretch - they are useful in 'freeing' the joint at its maximum range of movement.

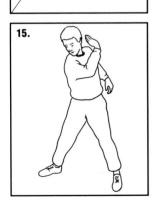

15.

• Skipping makes an ideal warm-up exercise (but stretch the calves first if they are cold) or training activity. It has aerobic and local muscle endurance benefits as well as being good for coordination. Encourage skipping with alternate feet as this is more akin to running, and as soon as they are competent get them doing doubles (two turns of the rope at each jump). Record the number of skips in one minute etc.

• Stretching is an essential part of the warm-up, as we have seen, and stretching on a regular (ideally daily) basis is valuable to all players. Some are illustrated on pages 90-92, beginning at the top of the body and working downwards. Stretches should be done slowly, held for the count of ten and then repeated; make sure both sides of the body are stretched.

• Ghosting is useful in the development of movement skills, as described in Chapter 3, and there is an inevitable attendant training benefit. A five minute 'float' ghost, although done very slowly, puts significant demands on the leg (local muscle endurance) and the simple circuit in Chapter 3, can be done fast for some anaerobic value. To put greater emphasis on agility, a shot/counter-shot version of the circuit can be used; after each shot, the player takes two strides back towards the 'T' and then goes back to repeat the shot. Or along similar lines, players ghost, playing one shot at the first position to which they go, two at the next, three at the third etc. Thus a ten-shot /counter-shot circuit race involves a total of fifty-five shots/movements. As well as the first-to-finish winner, the coach can select a champion according to style/quality.

Circuit training

Circuit exercises are relatively safe, even for children, because they involve using the body's own weight as resistance. They must be done exactly as shown, however, and should not be performed until fatigue causes a dangerous deterioration in quality. Often, youngsters find circuit exercises hard to coordinate, in which case get them to do them slowly merely to perfect the movement/improve coordination. Avoid any exercises which are evidently too demanding, and again discourage young pupils from doing too much too often. An occasional session will help strength, and have an aerobic and anaerobic (if they are able to go fast) benefit; from the coach's point of view, it is another way of profitably occupying off-court time.

Swap and run

To introduce plenty of exercise, and to encourage all players to keep the score and compete for every point, I get them to swap scores, winner with loser, at the end of a routine or conditioned game. They then have to run that number of court-widths (running side to side, touching the nick). Done properly, there is plenty of leg/back/abdominal strengthening because of the lunge and turn involved.

Note: Excuse any player with a knee soreness.

Time trials

Running lengths of the court is good exercise, but boring, so the introduction of a target time can offer a more interesting challenge. With young players, 20 lengths in one minute is a suitably demanding target. This can be stepped up to 30 in ninety seconds for stronger pupils, or 50 in two-and-a-half minutes, and, ultimately, 100 in five minutes. Time-trials are something of a test of character as well as aerobic fitness.

Relay races

Relay races always create excitement and, by introducing ghosting and racket work in that order, are even more beneficial. There are all sorts of permutations, but a typical race is shown. Choose two captains and let them select their own teams. With a ball in their hands, start off the first two players from the door in a race through the five-shot ghosting routine. They should then play a certain number of the selected shots before handing the ball on to the next player in the team. Time the difference between the two teams, change the side of court they use, and repeat to get an overall winner. By varying the number and the choice of shots, and the number of times each member goes through the sequence, the race can be infinitely varied in terms of difficulty and duration. Races make an ideal finale.

Physiological points to note

• Children have a greater capacity for, and derive more benefit from, aerobic exercise; they are not so well-equipped for anaerobic/explosive type work.
• Children breathe faster and less deeply than adults during exercise because their immature system is less efficient at extracting oxygen. Consequently, their water loss is greater, so coaches should be understanding in allowing 'time-out' for drinks.

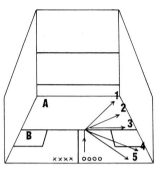

RACKET SKILLS
A 10 ANGLE VOLLEYS
B 10 SHOTS TO SERVICE BOX

1 DROP
2 VOLLEY DROP
3 VOLLEY LENGTH
4 STRAIGHT DRIVE
5 BOAST

NOTE
RACKET SKILLS AND GHOSTING ARE SHOWN ON SEPARATE SIDES ONLY FOR CLARITY - BOTH TEAMS DO BOTH ACTIVITIES.

Summary

Concentrate on racket skills with beginners, using safe training ideas to occupy off-court time, and remember that children must **not** be given a hard training programme.

6

SPEAKING FROM EXPERIENCE ...

Speaking from Experience...

Every coach evolves his own methods for dealing effectively with groups of beginners, but it takes time. Hopefully the following thoughts may go some way to speeding up the evolutionary process.

Planning a Session

Aims and scope

Group coaching is inevitably a compromise. The coach cannot expect equal and perfect progress from every pupil, but neither should he shirk the challenge of achieving at least some improvement with every player. Coaching groups is exciting because it offers the best vehicle for teaching as much as possible to as many as possible.

Session format

Notwithstanding the need for flexibility, I utilize a basic format for group or squad work:

1. Pre warm-up racket skills

A gentle racket skill exercise which may revise or re-test something from the previous session. It means immediate activity and can easily absorb late arrivals.

2. Warm-up

Not only a physical preparation but a chance to remember names, set the scene for the session etc.

3. Solo racket-practice

Whenever possible I like to get everyone involved on an individual basis right away. Having warmed up, players should keep warm and, having perhaps watched a demonstration, they will be itching to have a go. Don't forget to record scores.

4. Pairs practice

Feeding and practice, competition between pairs rallying cooperatively or between competing individuals. Maximum activity using both sides of the court.

5. Conditioned games, competitive routines or matches
With only two players on court, or groups using three-quarters of
the court, with any spare players fully occupied off court.

6. Finale
All players back on court for a vigorous end to the session, ideally
involving fairly strenuous exercise along with racket skills (as
discussed in Chapter 5).

7. Warm-down and summary
The warm-down can be done off court if necessary (making
maximum use of court time to actually play) and it is an ideal time
to summarize the lesson with special reference to practices which
should be repeated before the next session.

8. Chat to parents
There will always be some parents there waiting to know how
their offspring are progressing. Make time to tell them, good or
bad.

Planning a Course

Situations vary but a twelve-week course is suitable for covering
the basic shots of the game. It should enable the better pupils to
grasp the essential requirements so they can play a game
competently by the end. The balance between progression and
perfection has to err towards keeping the quicker learner interested
and stretched, but there must be constant revision in order to
consolidate. Here is a suggested course outline:

Week 1 - Assessment and basic racket control.
Week 2 - Straight drives and an introduction to the idea of length.
(Pupils can start the rally with a drive in order to play a game or
they can quickly be shown a proper serve.)
Week 3 - Straight volleys to length.
Week 4 - Service and return of service (this is easier if the volley
has already been covered.)

Week 5 - Boast. The easiest way of overcoming the biggest problem: how to get the ball out of the back corners.

Week 6 - Straight drop. An ideal complement to the length shot.

Week 7 - Tournament and an introduction to marking and refereeing. Games on a round-robin basis, showing them how to write down the score and explaining the basic points of the Let/ Stroke rule, stressing the safety aspect and highlighting basic tactics.

Week 8 - Straightening. An even better way than the boast for getting out of the back corners.

Week 9 - Straight volley drop

Week 10 - Cross-court length. Drives and volleys with width as well as length.

Week 11 - Lobs (cross-court first).

Week 12 - Tournament, ideally with a proper draw sheet, a plate even (to keep everyone involved) and perhaps some modest prizes not just for the winners but also the most sporting or best behaved, the most improved, the best marker and, possibly, best-behaved parent!

Notes: This schedule assumes a two-hour session each week. Successful progress along these lines will be very much dependent upon the grasping of the racket-control work at the very beginning. Simple tactical ideas can be introduced as appropriate throughout the course and players should be encouraged to practise between sessions.

The course outlined is intended primarily to suggest a sequence of events taking twelve weeks as a typical period. Ideally, much more time should be spent on each stage , especially the first two, but if the coach is compelled to condense things the schedule given ensures that even the most able player is continually stretched, and that all players will have some knowledge of the essential elements of the game at the end. Hopefully, they will continue to attend an Improvers' course, where the appropriate revision/consolidation can take place.

Safety factors

Safety must be stressed if accidents are to be avoided - with groups of racket-wielding beginners especially. Anticipating that the worst is always possible, the coach should know where the nearest first-aid kit is and also where to find some ice. The following safety points should be made very clear to pupils from their first lesson; when a little apprehension may help attention.

1. Never walk on to court without knocking.

2. The racket can be a lethal weapon and the ball a potential bullet, so beware.

3. Never hit the ball towards the back of the court or deliberately towards someone, even in fun.

4. Perfect a safe follow-through as soon as possible (and certainly before you run out of people who will play with you!).

5. Try to be aware of the other players on court, especially when serving from the 'T' in alley games.

6. Never leave rackets or balls lying around on the floor, especially for the swap and run exercise.

7. It is vital to listen carefully to all instructions and then do exactly as asked, especially when the coach has to leave to go to another court. Jump on any players who decide to change activities as soon as you close the door.

8. Make reference to the let and stroke situation from the very beginning (you can expand upon it later). Stress that you never play the ball if you suspect that racket or ball may endanger your opponent.

9. Generally concentrate on accuracy before power, since it is usually the wild shots which do the damage.

Notes

There will always be one or two players who never seem to take in instructions. Apart from being annoying, they are potentially dangerous when sent off in a group to another court, so get to know who they are as early as possible and try to use them to repeat your instructions at the end of an explanation.

Any infringement of safety rules should meet with a stern warning and any repetition should lead to dismissal from the court - even if it does mess up the convenient, even number of players.

Plan it

Plan each session in as much detail as possible but be careful to build in some flexibility so the lesson doesn't flounder because numbers are different from those predicted. List methods of scoring and timings for each phase, and have necessary score-sheets already prepared. It is useful to have an extra activity up your sleeve just in case there is time to spare, although the opposite is far more likely. If the coach is absolutely clear what he is doing, he is much more likely to be confident and relaxed, in which case he will coach better. The written preparation for each session then becomes a record of what has been covered. This can be very useful if the coach is doing similar courses with different groups and for making additional notes on particular successes or failure for future reference. It is valuable to be able to see at a glance exactly what you did the previous session. If you can't remember, how can you expect your pupils to?

Controlling groups

Get them all standing or sitting together and make it plain from the start that you expect silence when the coach is speaking, and that they should listen intently to all instructions before asking questions. Ask questions constantly in order to keep them on their toes. It also helps to keep slipping individual names into the explanation and instructions to give the impression that this particular gem of wisdom is aimed specifically at the player who is paying least attention. Always have a final check that they know what they are doing and where they are going before they start.

Maximum activity

Try to keep everyone occupied all the time if at all possible. Those having to wait on court for their turn can always be asked to count, score and analyse technique seeing their mistakes in others. Whilst waiting off-court, players can mark or referee and carry out some form of analysis (just recording unforced errors is always useful), do some light training activity or even have a quiet drink.

Time it

Keep a stopwatch handy. It makes for much smoother control if each activity is run for a certain time rather than to a score, so each group stay in phase.

Coach, don't just occupy them

Although carefully chosen, well-explained practices will almost guarantee improvement to some degree, it is still vital for the coach to correct errant technique, and witness and praise improvement before moving on to the next court. If need be, actually grip the pupil's racket with him and tell him to relax so you can take him through the stroke and give him the feel of the correct swing. If a factor is a general problem, get the whole group together so as to explain it once only. With a large group, particularly if not too receptive, it is easy for us coaches to fall into the trap of thinking that to occupy pupils is sufficient. It is not. They must be occupied profitably and must be coached at every opportunity.

Get on to court

Although it is easier to keep a general eye on things from the balcony and off-court, it is much more effective to coach from on-court, because players can hear you better and are better motivated by having you on the spot. Standing against the back wall is safe and unobtrusive.

Coach feeding

As far as possible I like players to feed for each other because it is good practice for them and it leaves me free to coach on the move. However, if the quality of the practice is falling victim to poor-quality feeding, it is useful for the coach to stop and feed, coaching as he does so. He may feed for the whole group using the whole court, or feed on one side only whilst practice continues on the other half of the court.

Loads of praise

If the coach notices a good shot, or even just a good try, he should never miss the chance to praise it. Everyone appreciates recognition of their efforts (not just their successes).

Attention to detail

Insist on exactly what you are after in terms of technique. Regard it as an admission of defeat if you fail to get a pupil to do it right.

Just because a pupil's faulty technique is familiar to you, don't turn a blind eye to it. Keep correcting it until you win, then he might too. Emphasize at all times that quality counts above all else, even in competition.

Make it competitive

Notwithstanding the quest for quality, once the essence of a new skill has been grasped, competition is valuable whenever possible. American scoring makes every rally count and highlights losing shots as well as the winners. Competition helps concentration.

Record scores

Keep a record of scores on practices so you can re-test, telling players what their target is beforehand, and confirming improvement or otherwise afterwards. If you have asked them to keep the score, try not to forget to ask them what the score was at the end of the practice. Use the scores - the swap and run idea has already been mentioned; an alternative is simply to ask players to subtract their score from the number you determine and they do that number of squat-thrusts, court-widths etc. Make fun of the scores, so the poor lad who has the most to do doesn't feel too bad about it and anyone who ridicules him is volunteering to join him!

Sorting into ability groups

Group according to ability rather than age or size when the activity is skill-based. Use the results of a skill test or if going in 'blind', use a 3/4-court game or alley game (see Chapter 4). With say, four courts, number every player 1,2,3,4 ; 1,2,3,4 etc down the line as they stand and make all the 1s start on court 1 etc. Let them play for four minutes, after which the winners move up a court to the right and the losers move down to the left. Have sufficient changes for those who were forced to start at the bottom to reach the 'superstar' court, and in the case of the 3/4-court game, remember to alternate service side with each change. Rather than call them group one, or top and bottom, name them after the top players in the world. That way even the bottom group can identify themselves with the world's fourth best player and their pride is preserved.

Coping with awkward numbers

Inevitably numbers vary from week to week or even within a single group-session as players arrive late, or have to leave early, so the coach must be able to adapt his carefully-laid plans. The following suggestions may help:

• **Odd numbers** - the easy answer is for the coach to join in. Pupils like this, but it is important to keep swapping opponents, partners and courts to see as many players as possible.

• **Three players** - if a two-ball feed is not appropriate, ask the loser of each rally to drop out of play and the third player to step in.

• **Five players** - this is actually the perfect number for any alley game. One player stands against the door ready to take the place of the first player to lose a rally. The loser then drops out and waits to replace the next loser etc. Each player keeps his own score. This arrangement has the advantage of ensuring that players play on both sides of the court against a variety of opponents.

• **Up to six players (or even more)** - any variation on the three-quarter court game (or half-court and front-court) which leaves some part of the court free and safe for those waiting will work well with a group. I would let the winner stay on with a maximum of, say, five consecutive points to prevent total domination by one player. This arrangement can safely accommodate more than six players although there is then too much waiting for it to be ideal.

Be fair

As well as the more obvious points - such as dividing your time evenly, and showing no favouritism - the coach must be seen to be fair in such matters as court allocation. If there is an exhibition court or one with a preponderance of smelly black mould, do rotate the group for, however unreasonable it may seem to the best players, the 'no-hopers' would appreciate a turn on the best court. Who knows, they may be inspired.

Feeding as a skill

In pairs practice there is a tendency for the player who is feeding to feel he is just killing time until it is his go. The coach should stress that consistently-accurate feeding is often more demanding than the practice itself. To reinforce this he should be ready to praise success at both. In short, try as a coach to generate in your players a pride in feeding well and maybe give an award to the best feeder.

Make it fun

Last, but certainly by no means least, try to make the session fun. Although you are working and have certain skills to impart, remember it is your players' recreation so do have a laugh and make learning fun - after all, if they don't enjoy your sessions, they won't come back for more.

Summary

• Aim to achieve some success with every player in the group
• Decide on a basic format or structure to your group sessions
• Remember to chat to parents
• Plan a course over a finite period
• Stress safety factors right from the start
• Plan each session in as much detail as possible and use the plan as a record of what has been done
• Try to control groups efficiently so as not to waste time
• Incorporate maximum activity into each session and try to ensure that everyone is occupied all the time
• Time each phase of the session so you have control
• Coach the players, don't just occupy them
• Get on to court to coach whenever possible
• Feed the ball yourself if necessary and join in if extra motivation or demonstration is needed
• Praise whenever the opportunity arises
• Pay attention to detail and insist on quality
• Use competition whenever - possible providing it is not compromising quality
• Keep a record of scores, times etc
• Sort into groups according to ability for skill work
• Think in advance how you will cope with awkward numbers
• Be fair about court allocation, division of time etc
• Try to develop a pride in feeding well
• Try to make learning fun.

Coaching the Individual

In almost every way, coaching on an individual basis holds nothing but advantage over the group situation and many coaches relish the one-to-one ratio. Progress ought to be more rapid, and it is much easier to perfect things with just one player. However, there are three factors to which I shall draw attention.

Relaxing a pupil

Remember that, unlike the group session, the individual lesson offers no anonymity, no chance to hide at the back and possibly because of this some players are very nervous. The coach should try to put the pupils at ease with a friendly, encouraging manner. However unsuccessful a player's first attempts might be, assure him that you have experienced much worse (even if you have to lie a bit). Try to ensure that he achieves some success so you have something to praise and then, hopefully, a certain amount of confidence will develop.

Assessment

Start by actually asking a player how much squash he has played, if any, and enquire if he plays other racket games. If he knows the basic rules and can obviously hit the ball have a quick knock-up and play a game or two with him. Tell him not to try to do anything special otherwise there is a danger that every other shot will go into the tin as he strives for impossible winners. If he is a true beginner, no assessment is really necessary so begin with work on the grip, basic racket control and drive technique -the beauty of the individual lesson being that progression can be geared exactly to the pupil.

Use of notes

As with group coaching, I find it essential to write notes on each session. The notes form a record of what was covered, the teaching points most relevant to that pupil and the practices which should be worked upon before the next lesson. In fact, I take eight to ten minutes at the end of the lesson to write these notes with the pupil, asking him questions to see what he has taken in. He then takes the notes to study whilst I retain a carbon copy for my records. There is then no excuse for his forgetting what was said, and he has the notes to take on to court with him when he practises. I realize that some.coaches will be cursed with short lessons which render this approach impracticable, or they may regard the time as better spent hitting the ball, but even so, a few notes jotted down afterwards just for the coach's benefit should help the logical planning of the next lesson.

Summary
• Try to relax your pupil at the start of a lesson
• Assess a new pupil by asking him about his squash, then playing a game if possible, or beginning basic racket-control coaching if not
• Use coaching notes in order to chart progress and plan future lessons.

The First Match or Tournament

It is difficult to say when beginners are no longer beginners because improvement is a gradual and continuous process and good players never really stop learning. Readiness for a match, however, requires the player to have basic competence, although there is still much refining of technique and tactical acumen to come.

Let us imagine that a twelve-week beginners' course is to culminate in an internal tournament, or a match against another club or sports centre with a similar group of players. For the coach, this match may be very informal, but for the beginner it may well be the most important day of his squash career so far.

Coping with nerves
Solo games like squash are likely to generate more competitive stress than team games, and the more doubt a player has about his

ability to cope with the situation, the greater the likely stress. With many children the problem is not in motivating them but in removing the fear of failure. The coach can attempt to do this by playing down the importance of the result, telling the apprehensive player to simply go out and enjoy himself. With this in mind it may well be necessary for the coach of a younger pupil to have a word with the over-zealous parent, pointing out as tactfully as possible that to lean too heavily on their offspring is to jeopardize his continued enjoyment of the game and consequently his future participation.

Tactics

It can help a player no end to have a simple plan clear in his head when he steps on to court. For instance, with a junior beginner, I would advise him. 'If in doubt, hit the ball high and straight to length and play a straight drop whenever you have the chance'. The act of thinking positively about a strategy can help to take the mind off being nervous.

Learn from defeat

Pre-match fear of losing and post-match frustrations can be minimized by acknowledging that often more is to be learned from defeat than victory and that it is quite possible to play very well, yet lose to a better opponent. Although winning will always be more enjoyable, if the coach can persuade his pupils that losing can be valuable in showing up weaknesses to be worked on in the future, he can help them to come to terms with disappointment. Try to get them thinking positively about why they lost.

Behaviour

Last, but perhaps most important of all, coaches have to take responsibility for teaching young players how to behave on court. It has to be made clear that racket-banging, swearing, arguing, kicking the wall and crying on court are unacceptable and cannot be tolerated. I like to approach the issue by trading on the pupil/coach relationship which one hopes has developed. I explain that they let me down when they lose their temper, and try gradually to generate a pride in remaining in control at all times. Aggression should be directed at the ball and not at those unfortunate enough to be around at the time. I like to think that good habits formed young with guidance from the coach will, with any luck, mature with the player and make the game as a whole even more pleasant.

Summary

• Try to minimize stress and remove the fear of losing by reminding players that it is only a game.
• Arm players with a simple plan before they go on to court.
• Help them to think positively and to learn from defeat.
• Set and insist on high standards of behaviour.

So the beginners have just successfully graduated with the conclusion of their first match. Time for the coach to settle back with his well-earned drink, and reflect contentedly upon their mutual achievements. No time for complacency however: the courts are booked for next week, and there are sixteen names on the list ... you have to do it all over again!

Happy coaching.

RULES OF SQUASH

RULES OF SQUASH

RULES OF THE INTERNATIONAL SINGLES GAME

THE FOLLOWING RULES ARE AS PUBLISHED BY THE SQUASH RACKETS ASSOCIATION.

CONTENTS

1. THE GAME

The game of Squash Rackets is played between two players, each using a standard racket, with a standard ball and in a court constructed to ISRF standard dimensions.

2. THE SCORE

A match shall consist of the best of three or five games at the option of the organisers of the competition. Each game is to nine points, in that the player who scores nine points wins the game except that, on the score being called eight-all for the first time, the receiver shall choose, before the next service is delivered, to continue that game either to nine points (known as 'No Set') or to ten points (known as 'Set Two'), in which latter case the player who scores two more points wins the game. The receiver shall in either case clearly indicate his choice to the marker, referee and his opponent.

The marker shall call either 'No Set' or 'Set Two' as applicable before play continues.

3. POINTS

Points can be scored only by the server. When the server wins a stroke, he scores a point; when the receiver wins a stroke, he becomes the server.

4. THE SERVICE

4.1 The right to serve first is decided by the spin of a racket. Thereafter the server continues to serve until he loses a stroke, whereupon his opponent becomes the server, and this procedure continues throughout the match. At the commencement of the second and each subsequent game, the winner of the previous game serves first.

4.2 At the beginning of each game and each hand, the server has the choice of either box and thereafter shall serve from alternate boxes while remaining the server. However if a rally ends in a let he shall serve again from the same box.

Note to Officials
If it appears that the server intends to serve from the wrong box, or either player appears undecided as to which is the correct box, the Marker shall advise the correct box. If the Marker makes an error with this advice or there is any dispute, the Referee shall rule on the correct box.

4.3 For a service to be good, there must be no foot-fault and the ball, before being struck, shall be dropped or thrown in the air and shall not hit the walls, floor, ceiling or any object suspended from the walls or ceiling; it shall be served direct onto the front wall between the cut line and the outline, so that on its return, unless volleyed, it reaches the floor within the back quarter of the court opposite to the server's box. Should a player, having dropped or thrown the ball in the air, make no attempt to strike it, the ball shall be dropped or thrown again for that service. A player with the use of only one arm may utilise his racket to propel the ball into the air before striking it.

4.4 A service is good when it does not result in the server serving his hand out (Rule 4.6).

4.5 A service is a fault:

4.5.1 If at the time of striking the ball the server fails to have part of one foot in contact with the floor within the service box without any part of that foot touching the service box line (called a 'foot-fault'). Part of the foot may project over this line provided that it does not touch the line.

4.5.2 If the ball is served onto or below the cut line but above the board.

4.5.3 If the first bounce of the ball, unless volleyed, is on the floor on or outside the short or half court lines of the back quarter of the court opposite to the server's box.

4.6 The server serves his hand out and loses the stroke:

4.6.1 If he serves a fault.

4.6.2 If the ball after being dropped or thrown for service touches the walls, floor, ceiling or any object(s) suspended from the walls or ceiling before being served.

4.6.3 If the server makes an attempt but fails to strike the ball.

4.6.4 If, in the opinion of the referee, the ball is not struck correctly.

4.6.5 If the ball is served onto or below the board, or out, or against

any part of the court before the front wall.

4.6.6 If the ball, after being served and before it has bounced more than once on the floor, or before it has been struck at by the receiver, touches the server or anything he wears or carries.

4.7 The server must not serve until the Marker has completed calling the score.

Note to Officials
The Marker must not delay play by the calling of the score. However, if the server serves, or attempts to serve, prior to the calling of the score, the Referee shall stop play and require the server to wait until the calling of the score has been completed.

5. THE PLAY
After a good service has been delivered the players return the ball alternately until one fails to make a good return, the ball otherwise ceases to be in play in accordance with the rules, or on a call by the Marker or Referee.

6. GOOD RETURN

6.1 A return is good if the ball, before it has bounced more than once upon the floor, is returned correctly by the striker onto the front wall above the board, without first touching the floor or any part of the striker's body or clothing, or the opponent's racket, body or clothing, provided the ball is not hit out.

6.2 It shall not be considered a good return if the ball touches the board before or after it hits the front wall and before it bounces on the floor, or if the racket is not in the player's hand at the time the ball is struck.

7. LET

A let is an undecided stroke. The rally in respect of which a let is allowed shall not count and the server shall serve again from the same box.

8. STROKES

A player wins a stroke:

8.1 Under Rule 4.6, when the player is the receiver.

8.2 If the opponent fails to make a good return of the ball, unless a let is allowed or a stroke is awarded to the opponent.

8.3 If the ball touches his opponent or anything he wears or carries when his opponent is the non-striker, except as is otherwise provided by Rules 9, 10 and 13.1.1.

8.4 If a stroke is awarded to him by the Referee as provided for in the Rules.

9. HITTING AN OPPONENT WITH THE BALL

If the ball, before reaching the front wall, hits the striker's opponent or his racket, or anything he wears or carries, the ball shall cease to be in play and:

9.1 Unless Rule 9.2 applies, the striker shall win the stroke if the ball would

struck the front wall without first touching any other wall.

9.2 If the ball would have struck any other wall and would have made a good return but the striker has either followed it to pass around him - in either case by striking the ball to the right of the body after the ball had passed to his left (or vice versa) then a let shall be allowed in all cases.

Note to Referees.

If the striker, having turned or allowed the ball to pass around him, chooses not to continue the rally due to the reasonable fear of striking his opponent, and, in the opinion of the Referee, would have been able to make a good return then a let shall be allowed.

9.3 If the ball had struck or would have struck any other wall and would have made a good return, a let shall be allowed unless, in the opinionm of the Referee, a winning return has been intercepted, in which case the striker shall win the stroke.

9.3 If the ball had struck ar would have struck any other wall and would have made a good return, a let shall be allowed unless, in the opinion of the Referee, a winning return has been intercepted, in which case the striker shall win the stroke.

Notes to Referees

The stroke award provisions of Rule 9 do not apply to turning , ball passing around the striker, or further attempt.

9.4 If the ball would not have made a

good return the striker shall lose the stroke.

Notes to Officials

When a player has been struck by the ball as described in Rule 9, the marker shall call 'down'. The referee shall assess the trajectory of the ball and make all further decisions.

10. FURTHER ATTEMPTS TO HIT THE BALL.

If the striker strikes at and misses the ball, he may make further attempts to strike it. If, after being missed, the ball touches his opponent or his racket, or anything he wears or carries, then if, in the opinion of the Referee:

10.1 The striker could otherwise have made a good return, a let shall be allowed, or

10.2 The striker could not have made a good return, he loses the stroke. If any such further attempt is successful resulting in a good return being prevented from reaching the front wall by hitting the striker's opponent or anything he wears or carries, a let shall be allowed in all circumstances. If any such further attempt would not have made a good return, then the striker shall lose the stroke.

11. APPEALS

An appeal may be made against any decision of the marker.
Appeals to the Referee under Rule 11 should be prefaced with the words 'Appeal please'.

Play shall then cease until the referee has given his decision.
If an appeal under Rule 11 is disallowed, the marker's decision shall stand. If the Referee is uncertain he shall allow a let except where provided for in Note to Referees on Rule 11.2.1. and Notes to Referees C and D after Rule 11.2.2.
Appeals upheld or Referee intervention under Rule 20.4 are dealt with in each specific situation below.

Note to Referees
A pointing gesture during a rally is not a recognised form of appeal.

11.1 Appeals on service.

11.1.1 If the Marker calls 'fault', 'foot-fault', 'not up', 'down' or 'out' to the service the server may appeal. If the appeal is upheld a let shall be allowed.

11.1.2 If the marker fails to call 'fault' or 'foot-fault', 'not up', 'down' or 'out' to the service the receiver may appeal, either immediately or at the end of the rally if he has played or attempted to play the ball. If, in the opinion of the Referee, the service was not good he shall stop play immediately and award the stroke to the receiver.

11.2 Appeals on Play Other Than Service

11.2.1 If the marker calls 'not up','down' or 'out' following a player's return the player may appeal. If the appeal is upheld the Referee shall allow a let except that if, in the opinion of the Referee:

-The Marker's call has interrupted that player's winning return he shall award the stroke to the player.

- The Marker's call has interrupted or prevented a winning return by the opponent, he shall award the stroke to the opponent.

Note to Referees
In the latter case the Referee shall also award the stroke to the opponent if he is unsure whether the Marker's call was correct.

11.2.2 If the marker calls 'not up', 'down' or 'out' following a player's return the opponent may appeal either immediately, or at the end of the rally if he has played or attempted to play the ball. If, in the opinion of the Referee, the return was not good he shall stop play immediately and award the stroke to the opponent.

Notes to Referees
A. No appeal under Rule 11 may be made delivery of a service for anything that occurred before that service.
B. Where there is no more than one appeal in a rally (including an appeal under Rule 12) the Referee shall consider each appeal.
C. If a return is called 'not up', 'down' or 'out' by the Marker and that same return subsequently goes down or out the Referee, on appeal, if he reverses the Marker's call or is unsure, shall then rule on the subsequent occurrence.
D. If a service is called 'fault', 'foot fault', 'not up', 'down' or 'out' by the Marker and that service subsequently

goes down, not up or out, or is again a fault, the Referee, on appeal, if he reverses the Marker's call or is unsure, shall then rule on the subsequent occurrence

12. INTERFERENCE

12.1 After playing a ball, a player must make every effort to get out of his opponent's way. That is:

12.1.1 A player must make every effort to give his opponent a fair view of the ball.

12.1.2 A player must make every effort not to obstruct his opponent in the latter's direct movement to the ball. At the same time the opponent must make every effort to get to, and where possible play the ball.

12.1.3 A player must make every effort to allow his opponent freedom to play the ball.

Note to Referees
The freedom to play the ball must include a reasonable backswing, strike at the ball and a reasonable follow-through.

12.1.4 A player must make every effort to allow his opponent freedom to return the ball directly to the front wall

If a player fails to fulfil one of the requirements of Rule 12.1 (1 to 4) above, whether or not he has made every effort to do so, then interference will have occurred.

12.2 If any interference has occurred, and in the opinion of the Referee, the player has not made every effort to avoid causing it, the Referee shall on appeal, or on stopping play without waiting for an appeal, award the stroke to his opponent, provided the opponent was in a position to make a good return.

Note To Referees

In all cases under Rule 12 where a let or stroke is desired an appeal should be made to the Referee with the words 'Let please'. The appeal should be immediate.

12.3 However, if interference has occurred but in the opinion of the Referee the player has made every effort to avoid causing it, and the opponent could have made a good return, the Referee shall on appeal, or on stopping play without waiting for an appeal, allow a let, except that if his opponent is prevented from making a winning return by such interference from the player, the Referee shall award the stroke to the opponent.

Notes to Referees

A. A player who plays on despite interference forfeits the right to appeal concerning that interference.

B. When a player creates his own interference, the Referee shall rule that interference has not occurred.

12.4 When, in the opinion of the Referee, a player refrains from playing the ball which, if played, would clearly have won the rally under the terms of Rule 9.1 or 9.3, he shall be awarded the stroke.

12.5 If either player makes unnecessary physical contact with his opponent, the referee may stop play, if it has not already stopped, and apply the appropriate penalty.

Notes to Referees

A. The words 'not to obstruct' in Rule 12.1.2. must be interpreted to include the case of an opponent having to wait for an excessive follow-through of the player's racket.

B. A player's excessive backswing may create interference when his opponent has made every effort to avoid such interference. In this case if the player appeals for a let he shall not be awarded the stroke.

C. When, in the opinion of the referee, a player's swing is excessive and is considered to be dangerous, the referee shall apply Rule 17.

13. LETS

In addition to lets allowed under other rules, lets may or shall be allowed in certain other cases.

13.1 A let may be allowed:

13.1.1 If, owing, to the position of the striker, the opponent is unable to avoid being touched by the ball before the return is made.

Note to Referees

This rule shall include the cases where the striker's position is in front of his opponent, making it difficult for the latter to see the ball; or where the striker allows the ball to pass close to him and the ball hits his opponent who is behind the striker. This is not, however, to be taken as conflicting in any way with the duties of the Referee under Rule 12.

13.1.2 If the ball in play touches any articles lying on the floor.

Note to Referee

The Referee shall ensure that no articles are placed on the floor by the players.

13.1.3 If the striker refrains from hitting the ball owing to a reasonable fear of injuring his opponent.

Note to Referee

This rule shall include the case of the striker wishing to play the ball on to the back wall.

13.1.4 If, in the opinion of the referee, either player is distracted by an occurrence on or off the court.

13.1.5 If, in the opinion of the Referee, a change in court conditions has affected the result of the rally.

13.2 A let shall be allowed:

13.2.1 If the receiver is not ready and does not attempt to return the service.

13.2.2 If the ball breaks during play.

13.2.3 If the Referee is asked to decide an appeal and is unable to do so.

13.2.4 If an otherwise good return has been made but the ball goes out of court on its first bounce.

13.3 If the striker appeals for a let under Rules 13.1 (2 to 5) above, in order for a let to be allowed he must have been able to make a good return. For a non-striker appeal under Rules

13.1.2, 13.1.4 and 13.1.5 this is not a requirement.

13.4 No let shall be allowed under Rules 13.1.3 and 13.2.1 if the striker attempts to play the ball but may be allowed under Rules 13.1.2, 13.1.4, 13.1.5, 13.2.2, 13.2.3 and 13.2.4.

13.5
13.5.1 An appeal by the player is necessary for a let to be allowed under Rules 13.1.3 (striker only), 13.1.4, 13.2.1 (striker only) and 13.2.3

13.5.2 An appeal by the player or Referee intervention without appeal is applicable to Rules 13.1.2, 13.1.5, 13.2.2 and 13.2.4.

13.5.3 Where a player is struck by the ball as decsribed in Rule 13.1.1 the Referee shall decide without appeal whether a let is to be allowed or the stroke awarded to the striker.

14. THE BALL.

14.1 At any time, when the ball is not in actual play, another ball may be substituted by mutual consent of the players, or on appeal by either player at the discretion of the Referee.

Note to Referees

Either player or the Referee may examine the ball at any time it is not in actual play, to check its condition.

14.2 If a ball breaks during play, it shall be replaced promptly by another ball.

Note to Referees

The referee shall decide whether or not a ball is broken.

14.3 If a ball has broken during play but this has not been established, a let for the rally in whch the ball broke shall be allowed if the server appeals prior to the next service, or if the receiver appeals prior to attempting to return that service.

Notes to Referees

If the receiver appeals prior to attempting to return service and, in the opinion of the Referee, the ball break occurred during that service, the Referee shall allow a let for that rally only, but if unsure he should allow a let for the previous rally.

14.4 The provisions of Rule 14.3 do not apply to the final rally of a game. Appeal in this case must be immediately after the rally.

14.5 If a player stops during a rally to appeal that the ball is broken only to find subsequently that the ball is not broken, then that player shall lose the stroke.

15. WARM UP

15.1 Immediately preceding the start of play, the Referee shall allow on the court of play a period of five minutes to the two players together for the purpose of warming up the ball to be used for the match.
  After two and a half minutes of the warm up, the Referee shall call 'Half Time' and ensure that the players change sides unless they mutually agree otherwise. The referee shall also

advise when the warm up period is complete with the call of 'Time'.

15.2 Where a ball has been substituted under Rule 14 or when the match is being resumed after considerable delay, the Referee shall allow the ball to be warmed up to playing condition. Play shall resume on the direction of the referee, or upon mutual consent of the players, whichever is the earlier.

Note to Referees

The referee must ensure that both players warm up the ball fairly (Rules 15.1 and 15.2). An unfair warm up shall be dealt with under the provision of Rule 17.

15.3 The ball may be warmed up by either player between games unless there is an objection by one of the players. In the case of an infringement the Referee shall apply Rule 17.

16. CONTINUITY OF PLAY

After the first service is delivered, play shall be continuous so far as is practical, provided that:

16.1 At any time play may be suspended, owing to bad light or other circumstances beyond the control of the players, for such period as the referee shall decide. The score shall stand.

If another court is available when the court originally in use remains unsuitable, the match may be transferred to it if both players agree, or as directed by the referee.

In the event of play being suspended

RULES OF SQUASH

for the day, the score shall stand unless both players disagree in which case the match will start again.

16.2 An interval of ninety seconds shall be permitted between all games. Players may leave the court during such intervals but must be ready to resume play by the end of the stated time. When fifteen seconds of the interval permitted between games are left, the Referee shall call 'Fifteen seconds' to advise the players to be ready to resume play. At the end of the interval the Referee shall call 'Time'.
By mutual consent of the players play may recommence prior to the expiry of the ninety-second time interval.
It is the responsibility of the players to be within earshot of the court to hear the calls of 'Fifteen seconds' and 'Time'.

Notes to Referees
A. Should one player fail to be ready to resume play when 'Time' is called, the referee shall apply the provisions of Rule 17.

B. Should neither player be ready to resume play when 'Time' is called, the referee shall apply the provisions of Rule 17 for both players.

16.3 If a player satisfies the Referee that a change of equipment, clothing or footwear is necessary, the player may leave the court. He is required to effect the change as quickly as possible and the Referee shall allow him a period not exceeding two minutes for this purpose. If the player fails to return within the allotted time

the Referee shall apply the provisions of Rule 17.

16.4 In the event of an injury to a player the Referee shall decide if it was:

16.4.1 Self-inflicted.

16.4.2 Accidentally contributed to or accidentally caused by his opponent,

16.4.3 Caused by the opponent's deliberate or dangerous play or action.

Notes to Referees
A. In 16.4.2 and 16.4.3 above, the Referee must determine that the injury is genuine.

B. The referee must not interpret the words 'accidentally contributed to or accidentally caused by' to include the situation where the injury to the player is as a result of that player occupying an unnecessarily close position to his opponent.
In Rule 16.4.1 above the Referee shall require the player to continue play; or concede the game, accept the interval and then continue to play; or concede the match.
In Rule 16.4.2 above the Referee shall allow reasonable time for the injured player to recover, having regard to the time schedule of the competition. By the end of this period of time the injured player must resume play or concede the match. The score at the time of injury shall stand except that if play is resumed on another day the match may start again if both players agree.
In Rule 16.4.3 above the referee

shall award the match to the injured party.

16.5 The Referee shall apply the provisions of Rule 17 to a player who, in his opinion, delays play unreasonably. Such delay may be caused by:

16.5.1 Unduly slow preparation to serve or receive service.

16.5.2 Prolonged discussion with the Referee.

16.5.3 Delay in returning to the court having left under terms of Rules 16.2 and 16.3.

17. CONDUCT ON COURT
If the referee considers that the behaviour of a player on court could be intimidating or offensive to an opponent, official or spectator, or could in any other way bring the game into disrepute the player shall be penalised.

Where a player commits any of the offences listed in the Rules 12.5, 15.2 and 15.3, 16.2, 16.3 or the ISRF Code of Conduct (Appendix 6.1), the following penalty provisions may be applied.

Warning by the Referee (called a Conduct Warning).
Stroke awarded to opponent (called a Conduct Stroke).
Game awarded to opponent (called a Conduct Game).
Match awarded to opponent (called a Conduct Match).

Notes to Referees

A. If the referee stops play to give a warning, a let shall be allowed.
B. If the referee stops a rally to award a conduct stroke then that stroke award becomes the result of the rally. If the Referee awards a conduct stroke at the conclusion of a rally, the result of the rally stands and the conduct stroke award is additional but without change of service box.
 A conduct stroke awarded at the end of a game shall be carried over to the next game.
C. If the Referee awards a game that game shall be the one in progress or the next game if one is not in progress, in which latter case the interval between games shall not apply. The offending player shall retain any points already scored in the game awarded.

18. CONTROL OF A MATCH

A match is normally controlled by a Referee, assisted by a Marker. One person may be appointed to carry out the functions of both Referee and Marker. When a decision has been made by the Referee, he shall announce it to the players and the Marker shall repeat it with the subsequent score.

Notes to Officials

A. Having only one official to carry out roles of both Marker and Referee is undesirable.
B. Players are not permitted to request a chnage of Marker or Referee. The Tournament Referee has sole right to replace a Marker or Referee before or after the commencement of a match.

19. DUTIES OF A MARKER

19.1 The Marker calls the play followed by the score, with the server's score first. He shall call 'fault', 'foot-fault', 'out', 'not up' or 'down' as appropriate, and shall repeat the Referee's decisions.

19.2 If a Marker makes a call the rally shall cease.

Note to Markers

If the marker is unsighted or uncertain he shall make no call.

19.3 If play ceases and the Marker is unsighted or uncertain he shall advise the players and shall call on the Referee to make a relevant decision: if the Referee is unable to do so a let shall be allowed.

19.4 The Marker calls 'Hand out' to indicate a change of server.

Note to Markers

Markers must use recognised marker's calls including when the rally has ceased (Appendix 1.2).

20. DUTIES OF A REFEREE

20.1 The referee shall allow or disallow appeals for lets and award strokes; make decisions where called for by the rules, including when a player is struck by the ball and for injuries, and shall decide all appeals, including those against the Marker's calls or lack of calls. The decision of the referee shall be final.

20.2. The Referee shall exercise control:

20.2.1 Upon appeal by one of the players.

20.2.2 As provided for in Rules 4,9,10,11,12,13,14,15,16,7,18 and 19.

20.2.3 The Referee shall not intervene in the Marker's calling of the score unless, in the opinion of the Referee, the score has been called incorrectly in which case he shall have the Marker call the correct score.

Note to Officials

Both the Marker and Referee are required to record the score.

20.4 The Referee shall not intervene in the Marker's calling of the score unless, in the opinion of the Referee, the Marker has made an error in stopping play or allowing play to continue, in which case the Referee shall immediately rule accordingly.

20.5 The Referee is responsible for ensuring that all rules relating to time are strictly enforced.

20.6 The Referee is responsible for ensuring that court conditions are appropriate for play.

20.7 The Referee may award a match to a player whose opponent fails to be present on court, ready to play, within ten minutes of the advertised time of play.

RULES OF SQUASH

APPENDIX 1.1

DEFINITIONS

ADJUDICATOR
A person responsible for the conduct of players and officials throughout the tournament.

APPEAL
A player's request to the Referee to consider an on or off court situation. 'Appeal' is used throughout the rules in two contexts:
(1) Where the player requests the referee to consider varying a Marker's decision and,
(2) Where the player requests the Referee to allow a let. The correct form of appeal by a player is 'Appeal please' or "Let please'.

ATTEMPT
The Referee shall decide what is an attempt to play the ball. An attempt is made when, in the opinion of the Referee, the striker has moved his racket towards the ball from his backswing position with the intention of making a good return.

BOARD
The Board is the lower horizontal line marking on the front wall, with the 'TIN' beneath it for the full width of the court.

BOX (SERVICE)
A square delineated area in each quarter court, bounded by part of the short line, part of the side wall and by two other lines and from within which the server serves.

COMPETITION
A championship, tournament, league or other competitive match.

CORRECTLY
The ball being hit by the racket (held in the hand) not more than once nor with prolonged contact on the racket.

CUT LINE
A line upon the front wall, the top edge of which is 1.83 metres (six feet) above the floor and extending the full width of the court.

DOWN
The expression used to indicate that an otherwise good return has struck the board or has failed to reach the front wall. ('Down' is used as a Marker's call.)

GAME
Part of a match, commencing with a service by server and concluding when one player has scored or been awarded nine or ten points (in accordance with the rules).

GAME BALL
The state of the score when server requires one point to win the game in progress. ('Game ball' is also used as a Marker's call.)

HALF-COURT LINE
A line set upon the floor parallel to the side walls, dividing the back of the court into two equal parts, meeting the 'Short line' at its midpoint, forming the T.

HALF-TIME
The midpoint of the warm up (also used as a referee's call).

HAND
The period from the time a player becomes server until he becomes receiver.

HAND-OUT
Condition when change of server occurs. ('Hand-out' is also used as a marker's call to indicate that a change of hand has occurred.)

MATCH
The complete contest between two players commencing with the warm up and concluding when both players have left the court at the end of the final rally. (Covers broken ball rule.)

MATCH BALL
The state of the score when the server requires one point to win the match. ('Match ball' is also used as a marker's call.)

NOT UP
The expression used to indicate that a ball has not been struck in accordance with the rules. 'Not up' covers all services or returns which are not good and are neither down nor out - with the exception of faults and foot-faults. ('Not up' is also used as a Marker's call.)

OUT
The expression used to indicate that a ball has struck the out line or a wall above such line or the roof, or has passed over any part of the roof (e.g. cross bars). ('Out' is also used as a Marker's call.)

OUT LINE

A continuous line comprising the front wall line, both side wall lines and the back wall line and marking the top boundaries of the court.

Note: When a court is constructed without provision of such a line i.e. the walls comprise only the area used for play, or without the provision of part of such a line (e.g. a glass back wall), and the ball in play strikes part of the horizontal top surface of such a wall and deflects back into court, such a ball is out. Because of the difficulty in ascertaining just where the ball strikes the wall, the decision as to whether such a ball is out should be made by observing the deflection back into court - an abnormal deflection indicating that the ball is out. This decision should be made in the normal manner by the Marker, subject to appeal to the referee.

POINT

A unit of the scoring system. One point is added to a player's score when he is server and wins a stroke.

QUARTER (COURT)

One half of the back part of the court which has been divided into two equal parts by the half court line.

RALLY

Series of returns of the ball, comprising one or more such returns. A rally commences with a service and concludes when the ball ceases to be in play.

REASONABLE BACKSWING

The initial action used by a player in moving his racket away from his body as preparation prior to racket movement forward towards the ball for contact. A backswing is reasonable if it is not excessive. An excessive backswing is one in which the player's racket arm is extended towards a straight arm position and/or the racket is extended with the shaft approximately horizontal. The Referee's decision on what constitutes a reasonable as distinct from excessive backswing is final.

REASONABLE FOLLOW-THROUGH

The action used by a player in continuing the movement of his racket after it has contacted the ball. A follow-through is reasonable if it is not excessive. An excessive follow-through is one in which the player's racket arm is extended towards a straight arm position with the racket also extended with the shaft horizontal - particularly when the extended position is maintained for other than a momentary period of time. An excessive follow-through is also one in which the arm extended towards a straight position takes a wider arc than the continued line of flight of the ball, even though the racket shaft is in the correct vertical position. The Referee's decision on what constitutes a reasonable versus excessive follow-through is final.

SERVICE

The method by which the ball is put into play by the server to commence a rally.

SHORT LINE

A line set out upon the floor parallel to and 5.49 metres (18 feet) from the front wall and extending the full width of the court.

STANDARD

The description given to balls, rackets and courts that meet existing ISRF specifications.

STRIKER

The player whose turn it is to hit the ball after it has rebounded from the front wall, or who is in the process of hitting the ball, or who - up to the point of his return reaching the front wall - has just hit the ball.

STROKE

The gain achieved by the player who wins a rally either in the course of play or on award by the referee and which results in either the scoring of a point or a change of hand.

TIN

The tin is situated between the board and the floor for the full width of the court and shall be constructed in such a manner as to make a distinctive noise when struck by the ball.

TOURNAMENT REFEREE

The Tournament Referee is given overall responsibility for all marking and refereeing matters throughout the tournament including the appointment and replacement of officials to matches.

GENERAL NOTE ONE

The use of the word 'shall' in the rules indicates compulsion and the lack of any alternative. The word 'must' indicates a required course of action

RULES OF SQUASH

with considerations to be taken into account if the action is not carried out. The word 'may' indicates the option of carrying out or not carrying out the action.

GENERAL NOTE TWO

When the words 'he', 'him' or 'his' are used in the rules, they shall be taken to mean 'she' and 'her' as appropriate.

APPENDIX 1.2

MARKER'S CALLS

The recognised Marker's calls are defined below.

Calls made by the Marker as referred to in:

RULES 19. DUTIES OF A MARKER

Fault To indicate that the service is a fault. See Rule 4.5.2 and 4.5.3.

Foot-Fault To indicate that the service is a foot-fault. See Rule 4.5.1.

Not Up To indicate that the ball has not been struck in accordance with the rules. See Definitions, 'NOT UP'.

Down To indicate that an otherwise good return has been struck the board or tin or has failed to reach the front wall. See Definitions, 'DOWN'.

Out To indicate that the ball has struck the out line or a wall above such line or the roof, or has passed over any part of the roof (e.g. cross bars). See Definitions, 'OUT'.

Hand Out To indicate that the server has become the receiver, i.e. a change of server has occurred. See Definitions, 'HAND OUT' and 'HAND'.

Calls made by the Marker as referred to in:

RULE 2. THE SCORE

4-3 An example of the score. The server's score is always called first, thus in this example the server leads by four points to three. If points are equal the wording used is 'all' (e.g. 'love-all').

No Set To indicate that the game in progress is to be played to nine points after the score has reached 8-all (called once only in any game).

Game Ball To indicate the server requires one point to win the game in progress. See Definitions, 'GAME BALL'.

Match Ball To indicate that the server requires one point to win the match. See Definitions, 'MATCH BALL'.

Calls made by the Marker as referred to in:

RULE 18. CONTROL OF A MATCH
(Repeating Referee Decisions)

Yes Let Calls made by the Marker after the Referee has ruled that a rally is to be replayed.

Stroke To (Name of Player) Call made by the Marker after the Referee

has awarded a stroke to that player.

No Let Call made by the Marker after the Referee has disallowed an appeal for a let.

Appendix 1.3
Referee's Calls

Stop To stop play.

Time To indicate that a period of time prescribed in the rules has elapsed.

Half-time To advise players of the mid-point of the warm up period.

Yes Let When allowing a let following a player's appeal for a let.

No Let When disallowing a player's appeal for a let.

Stroke to ... (Name of Player) To advise that the player named is to be awarded a stroke.

Fifteen seconds To advise the players that 15 seconds of the interval permitted between games remain.

Let (may be accompanied by an explanation). To advise that a rally is to be replayed in circumstances where the wording 'Yes Let' is not applicable.

Conduct Warning To advise a player that he has committed an offence under Rule 17. Conduct On Court, and is being given a warning.

Conduct Stroke To advise a player

that he has committed an offence under Rule 17. Conduct On Court, and that a stroke is to be awarded to his opponent.

Conduct Game To advise a player that he has committed an offence under Rule 17. Conduct On Court, and that a game is to be awarded to his opponent.

Conduct Match To advise a player that he has committed an offence under Rule 17. Conduct On Court, and that the match has been awarded to his opponent.

APPENDIX 2

DIMENSIONS OF A SQUASH COURT
Dimensions

Length .... 9.75 m (32 ft)
Breadth .... 6.40 m (21 ft)
Height to upper edge of cut line on front wall .... 1.83 m (6 ft)
Height to lower edge of front wall .... 4.57 m (15 ft)
Height to lower edge of back wall line .... 2.13 m (7 ft)
Distance to nearest edge of short line from back wall ... 4.26 m (13ft 10 in)
Height to upper edge of board from ground .... 0.48m (19 in)
Thickness of board (flat or rounded at top .. 12.5 mm (1/2 in) to 25.0 mm (1 in)
Height of side wall line: the diagonal line joining the front wall and back wall lines.

The service boxes shall be entirely closed on three sides within the court

by lines, the short line forming the side nearest to the front wall, the side wall bounding the fourth side.

The internal dimensions of the service boxes shall be 1.60 m (5ft 3in).

All dimensions in the court shall be measured from junction of the floor and front wall: 1 metre above the finished floor level.

All lines shall be 50 mm (2 ins) in width. All lines shall be coloured red.

In respect of the outer boundary lines on the walls, it is suggested that the plaster should be so shaped as to produce a concave channel along such lines.

Note
Further detailed information on squash courts is contained in the ISRF publication: 'Squash Courts Specification' (See ISRF Publications).

APPENDIX 3

DIMENSIONS OF A RACKET

1. Dimensions
Maximum length: 685 mm (27ins)
Maximum length: 215 mm (8.5 ins)
Maximum breadth:184 mm(7.25ins)
Framework of head:
Maximum width across the face .... 14 mm (0.56ins)
Maximum depth across the face .... 20 mm (0.81ins)
Maximum weight 255 gms (9 ozs)

Construction
At all times, the head or shaft shall not contain outside edges with a radius of curvature less than 2mm. Strings and string ends must be recessed within the racket head or, in cases where such recessing is impractical because of the racket material, or design, must be protected by a non-marking and securely attached bumper strip made of a flexible material which cannot crease into sharp edges following abrasive contact with floors and walls.

Strings shall be gut, nylon or a substitute material, providing metal is not used. Only two layers of string shall be allowed and these shall be alternately interlaced to form an othogonal array.

There should be no grommets, string spacers or other devices attached to any part of the strings wihtin the hitting area.

With effect from 1 January 1991, the frame of the racket shall be of a colour and/or material which will not mark the walls of the floor following an impact in normal play.

APPENDIX 4

SPECIFICATION OF A SQUASH BALL

The following ball specification is for the standard ISRF championship yellow dot ball

Mass (Weight) 23.2 to 24.6 gms.

Diameter 39.5 to 41.5 mm

Rebound The rebound test is performed on balls stabilised at 20° Centigrade using a sealed concrete floor surface. The percentage rebound is measured from the bottom of the ball.

Specification measurement 16 to 17%.

Deflection The deflection is measured as the meniscus (ink spot diameter) diameter shown when the ball is compressed under a load of 5.2kg between two glass plates.

Specification measurement 27.18 to 30.48 (1.07 to 1.2ins).

Seam Strength
Required seam strength for strength test is 2.54cms (1 in).
Seam strength is the load required to separate a 2.54cm length of seam. The load is applied normal to the seam and measured on a Scott Tensile Tester.

The load is gradually increased until the seam separates and the maximum load is recorded.

The minimum seam strength specification is 10.5kg/cm (60lbs/in). The average test result is 13.4kg/cm (75lbs/in).

APPENDIX 5

COLOUR OF PLAYERS' CLOTHING

Colours Organisers may specify regulations concerning players'

clothing which must be complied with in their particular tournament or tournaments.

APPENDIX 6.1

CODE OF CONDUCT

A player committing any of the following offences may be subject to penalty under Rule 17.

6.1.1 Verbal or physical abuse of his opponent, the Marker, Referee, officials, spectators or the sponsors.

6.1.2 Dissent to the Marker, Referee or officials, including foul or profane language and obscene or offensive gestures.

6.1.3 Abuse of playing equipment or the court.

6.1.4 Failure to comply with the rules or spirit of the game.

6.1.5 Any other unreasonable conduct which brings the game into disrepute.

APPENDIX 6.2

GUIDELINES FOR NATINAL FEDERATIONS, THEIR AFFILIATED ASSOCIATIONS AND TOURNAMENT ORGANISERS

Disciplinary committee:

A player who commits any of the following offences may be subject to disciplinary action by the disciplinary committee.

6.2. All offences listed in Appendix 6.1.

6.2.2 Failure to comply with the conditions of entry of a tournament including any rules with regard to clothing or advertising.

6.2.3 Withdrawal from an event or failure to attend after having entered a tournament or accepted an invitation to play.

6.2.4 Failure to complete a match.

6.2.5 Defaulting from a tournament or event. The disciplinary committee may require evidence or proof of 'bona fide' injury, illness or other emergency situation.

6.2.6 Failure by a player to make himself available to meet reasonable requests for interviews by the media.

1.1 Objects of the Disciplinary Committee

1.1.1 To uphold the good name of the I.S.R.F and the game.

1.1.2. To resolve all problems relating to conduct of players in their relations with each other, officials, sponsors and the public.

1.2 Powers of the Disciplinary Committee

1.2.1 To impose a warning or fine.

1.2.2 To withhold prize money from a player pending possible disciplinary action.

1.2.3 To recommend to the Officers of the Federation the banning of a player.

1.2.4 To recommend to the Officers of the Federation such action as may be necessary to uphold the objects of the disciplinary committee.

1.2.5 To send a full report to the National Association of the player concerned.

Procedures
2.1 Following the reporting of an incident to the disciplinary committee, a meeting shall be convened comprising the chairman of the disciplinary committee, an officer of the Federation, the player, and a representative of the player, if required by the player.

2.2 A player shall be notified of the likely charge to be made against him and shall be invited to submit his views to the ciommittee.

2.3 A player may appeal against the disciplinary action taken against him, but must do so within 28 days by notice in writing to the Federation.

2.4 An appeal will be heard by a select committee appoited by the Officers of the Federation.

Note: Member countries may adopt these guidelines for their own National Championships and other championships under the authority of the National Association, or use them as a basis for their own procedures.

RULES OF SQUASH

OFFICIAL GUIDELINES
Effective on 1st May 1989

INTRODUCTION

The over-riding principle governing the Rules of Squash and their Interpretation is to allow a fair result to each match. This requires that the Referee implements the Rules fairly for both players from the time the match starts to its final conclusion. The following Official Guidelines on Interpretations are those which have been discussed and approved by the Rules and Referees Committee of the ISRF and should be read in conjunction with the Rules.

G1. ONE SERVICE

This new concept is a fundamental change to the game of squash. However it is simple concept to understand and apply. All faults now result in a change of server and are the same as a fault on second service, or hand out on either service before the Rules were changed. Thus a foot fault becomes 'Hand out', as does a service which hits the front wall on or below the cut line or which lands in the incorrect quarter court. Servers will therefore need to concentrate more when serving. The change is designed to speed up play as well as making the Rules of service more easily understood.

G2. TURNING

With the deletion of the reference in Rule 9 to 'ball hitting the side wall' any situation in which a player turns and follows the ball round, or allows the ball to pass round his body, is now a potential 'Let' situation, i.e. if a player then stops and asks for a 'Let'

he cannot be given a 'Stroke'. However, the Referee, before allowing a Let, should be satisfied both that the striker would have been able to make a good return and that there was a reasonable possibility of the ball striking his opponent.

G3. MAKING EVERY EFFORT

The outgoing striker is required to make every effort to clear the ball after playing his return. His route should be on a path which allows the incoming striker direct access to the ball, provided the incoming striker has not moved in to play the ball so quickly that he blocks the outgoing striker's exit..

However, it is equally important for the incoming striker to make every effort to get to, and where possible, play the ball. If the incoming striker does not make every effort to get to the ball, then that is a significant factor in the Referee's assessment, of whether or not the player could have reached the ball and made a good return. The degree of effort that is required by the incoming striker, in order to demonstrate that he was indeed making every effort , is for the Referee to decide. Players should note that this does not give them licence to physically abuse their opponents and unnecessary physical contact will be penalised under Rules 12/17. A Referee, however, should not refuse Lets in situations where the player was clearly making every effort, (albeit short of physical contact with his opponent) to get to and play the ball and had demonstrated to the Referee that he would have reached the ball.

In giving his decision, the Referee must weight up the amount of effort being made by both players. In cases where the Referee assesses that sufficient effort has not been made by either player, he should take that into account when making his decision.

G4. APPEALS

A player who wishes to appeal under Rule 12 must do so immediately after the interference occurs. Play ceases at that point, if it has already done so. However, if a player's service or return immediately prior to his opponent's appeal, subsequently goes down or out, the Referee should not consider the appeal but rule on the service or return and award the stroke to the opponent.

An appeal under Rule 12 can be made only by the player whose turn it is to play the ball. When that player has completed his return, he then has no further right of appeal until it is once again his turn to play the ball. His protection against Unnecessary Physical Contact when it is his opponent's turn to play the ball is by Referee intervention under Rule 12.5.

G5 CREATED INTERFERENCE

At all times, a player must be allowed direct access to play the ball and his opponent, having competed his own return, must always endeavour to provide this direct access. However, sometimes the situation arises where the opponent has caused no interference (i.e. he clearly provided the required direct access) but the player has taken an indirect route to the ball which takes him through, or very close to, the opponent's position. He then appeals for a Let because he has been 'obstructed' in his access to the ball. But there is no genuine reason for this indirect route. In effect, he has 'created his own interference' where none otherwise existed and if he appeals for a Let he should not be allowed one. Whether he could have made a good return is not even a consideration; in order to remain in the rally, the player must get to and play the ball. This is not to be confused with two situations where a player in attempting to extricate himself from a position of disadvantage is denied direct access to the ball. The first is where a player is WRONG FOOTED, and anticipates his opponent hitting the ball one way, starts moving that way, but having guessed wrongly changes direction to find his opponent in the way. In this situation, he should be allowed a Let on appeal if he has recovered so as to show conclusively that he could have made a good return. In fact, had the incoming striker been prevented from playing a winning return, he may be awarded a 'stroke'. Secondly, if a player plays a poor return and he puts his opponent in a position of disadvantage, he should only be given a Let if, in taking the direct line to the ball for his next return he has shown conclusively that, but for the interference, he would have been able to get the ball.

G6 UNNECESSARY PHYSICAL CONTACT

Unnecessary physical contact is both detrimental to the game and potentially dangerous. In blatant cases, the Referee should stop the rally and award the appropriate penalty accordingly. The Referee should also be aware of a player who 'pushes off' his opponent. Where this has no significant effect on the opponent, then the rally should be allowed to continue and a warning given at the end of the rally.

G7 APPEALS FOR FEAR OF INJURY

When an appeal for a Let has been made and there has been no interference, the Referee's decision is usually 'No Let'. However, occasionally, although interference as defined in Rule 12.1 does not exist, there may be reasonable fear of injury in which case a let should be allowed under Rule 13.1.3.

G8 BROKEN BALL

When the receiver makes an appeal prior to attempting to return the service, the Referee has discretionary power to decide whether to replay the previous rally or to allow a Let in respect of the rally in which the ball was found to be broken.

G9 CHANGE OF EQUIPMENT

In order to avoid the situation of one player gaining an unfair rest interval through a change of equipment, the Referee should note that before allowing a player to leave the court to change equipment, the Referee must be satisfied that there has indeed been a material deterioration of the equipment. The preference for another racket, or a different pair of shoes where no physical deterioration is evident is not sufficient reason for allowing a change of equipment. The Referee should also note that although up to two minutes are allowed for a chnage of equipment, players are required to carry out the change as quickly as possible.

If a player loses a contact lens, or his glasses break, then following the appropriate time interval for a change of equipment, he must continue play or an appropriate Rule 17 penalty will be applied.

If a player is unable to resume play because he has no alternative equipment then the Referee should award the match to the opponent.

G10 ILLNESS/INJURY ON COURT

If, during a match, a player feels ill such that he needs to leave the court, then he must concede the game, take the game interval, then be ready to resume play. A player may concede only on game. If after taking the game interval, he is unable to continue play, he shall then concede the match. If, however, a player is sick on court, so that the court conditions are such that play is prevented from continuing, then the Referee should award the match to his opponent irrespective of whether the sick player is able to continue or not (Code of Conduct 6.1.3). Similarly, if a player suffers from a nose bleed and as a result, the

court conditions are impaired to the extent that they are detrimental to the match in progress, then his opponent should be awarded the match. (NB This refers to a 'natural' nose bleed rather than one caused by collision, where the relevant injury rule should apply.)

In all the above cases, the Referee's decision with regard to court conditions is final.

Players should note that where an injury is sustained which is entirely self-inflicted, including injury caused by a player being struck by his opponent's racket when the player has occupied an unnecessarily close position to the opponent, there is no statutory time interval for the player to recover. The Referee will require the player to continue, or concede the game, accept the interval and then continue to play or concede the match.

G11 TIME WASTING

Time wasting represent an attempt by one player to gain an unfair advantage over his opponent. Prolonged discussion with the Referee and slow preparation to serve or receive service are particularly mentioned (Rule 16.5). Where this is excessive, the Referee should warn the offending player at the earliest opportunity and thereafter penalise him with the award of a stroke, game or match to his opponent. It should be noted that while excessive ball bouncing prior to service does not constitute time wasting, the server should not be

considered to have served his hand out.

During game intervals, the Referee is required to call '15 seconds' to indicate that the players have 15 seconds to return to court and be ready to resume play. It is the responsibility of players to be within earshot to hear the call. A player who is not ready to resume play on the call of 'Time' is deliberately or otherwise gaining an unfair advantage and should be penalised under Rule 17.

G12 CODE OF CONDUCT/ PROGRESSION OF PENALTIES

The penalties available to the Referee under Rule 17 are:
A warning
A stroke
A game
The match

The guidelines for applying the penalties are as follows:
The first penalty imposed by the Referee for a particular offence may be at any level to suit the seriousness of the offence, i.e. a warning, stroke, game, or match. However, any second or subsequent penalty for the same type of offence may not be of a lesser severity than the previous penalty for that offence. Thus the Referee may award several warnings or several strokes for the same type of offence if he felt that the offence did not warrant a stronger punishment.

In issuing penalties, the Referee should use the following terminology:

Conduct warning ... (player's name) for ... (offence)

Conduct stroke ... (player's name) for ... (offence), stroke to ... (opponent's name)

Conduct game ... (player's name) for ... (offence), game to ... (opponent's name)

Conduct match ... (player's name) for ... (offence), match to ... (opponent's name).

G13 SINGLE OFFICIAL

It may not always be possible to have two officials for a match. A single official would act as the Marker initially, but when there was an appeal, he would then take on the Role of the Referee and give his decision, on appeal, as the Referee. Whilst this situation is not recommended, it does happen and the single official should know that he acts as the Marker, and then on appeal, the Referee. It is not correct to say that because there is only one official, there is no Referee.

G14 MARKER'S CALLS

The Marker must call to stop a rally if, in his opinion, a player has failed to deliver a good service or to make a good return. However, if because of a service or return which was obviously not good, both players

cease to play without the Marker making a call, then the appropriate call of 'not up', 'down' or 'out' may be omitted.

SHAPING THE BALL TO PLAY

A player who 'shapes' to play the ball on one side and then changes to play the ball on the other side should be allowed a Let if interference occurs. This is always assuming that he was not in a position to play a winning return and that his opponent was making every effort to move clear, otherwise the player should be awarded a stroke. This situation frequently occurs after the ball has hit the side/front wall nick. 'Shaping' to play the ball will normally mean some form of racket preparation but can be further extended to include any preparations, e.g. footwork, body position.

GENERAL
MARKER'S GUIDELINES

In general, the correct order of calls is:
1. Anything affecting the skin.
2. The score (with server's score always first).
3. Comments on the Score.

Examples are:
'Not up, hand out, 4-3.'
'Down, 8-all, no set, game ball.'
'Yes Let, 3-4.'
'No Let, hand out. 5-7.'

'Stroke to White, 8-2, match ball.'
'Foot fault, hand out, love-all.'
'Fault' (appeal by server, Referee unsure)'Yes Let,8-3, game ball.'

Match introduction:
'White serving, Black receiving, Best of 5 games, Love all.'

Start of subsequent game:
'Black leads one game to Love, Love all.'

Addressing the Players
It is recommended that Referees, when addressing the players, refer to male players by their surname with the prefix Mr., and to female players with the prefix Mrs, Miss or Ms. The use of first names should be avoided to eliminate any risk of familiarity with either player which could be interpreted as favouritism by the opponent.

Explanation by Referees
Following an appeal by a player, the referee will normally give his decision and play resumes. However, on some occasions it may be appropriate to explain the decision in order to clarify the situation for the players. Where the Referee feels this is appropriate, then he should give his decision followed by a concise and objective statement of explanation.

THIS BOOK HAS SHOWN THE IMPORTANT AND WIDE-RANGING ROLE OF THE COACH. IT HAS ALSO INDICATED THE KNOWLEDGE REQUIRED TO BE AN EFFECTIVE AND SUCCESSFUL COACH. THE SCOPE OF THIS BOOK CANNOT COVER EVERY TOPIC IN DETAIL, SO IF YOU HAVE DEVELOPED AN INTEREST IN SOME ASPECT OF COACHING SUCH AS MENTAL PREPARATION, FITNESS TRAINING OR THE PREVENTION OF INJURY, THE **NATIONAL COACHING FOUNDATION**, ESTABLISHED TO PROVIDE A SERVICE FOR SPORTS COACHES, RUNS COURSES, PRODUCES STUDY PACKS, BOOKS, VIDEOS AND OTHER RESOURCES ON MANY PERFORMANCE RELATED AREAS PARTICULARLY DESIGNED FOR THE PRACTISING COACH.

CONTACT THE **NATIONAL COACHING FOUNDATION** AT: 4 COLLEGE CLOSE, BECKETT PARK, LEEDS LS6 3QH. TELEPHONE: LEEDS (0532) 74802